TECHNICS AND CREATIVITY

TECHNICS AND CREATIVITY

Ⓘ GEMINI GEL

WITH AN ESSAY BY RIVA CASTLEMAN

THE MUSEUM OF MODERN ART, NEW YORK

*Text copyright ©1971 The Museum
of Modern Art, New York*

*Illustrations copyright ©1971
Gemini G.E.L., Los Angeles*

*Library of Congress Catalog Card
Number 79-150085 ISBN 0-87070-615-2*

Designed by John M. Coy

Printed by Graphic Press

*Photograph credits: All photographs
by Malcolm Lubliner except as listed.*

*Ed Cornachio: pp. 36-38, 53;
Catalogue Raisonné numbers 21- 22,
26-27, 29-32, 34, 46-47, 74-82,
87-90, 93-94, 96-133, 142-147, 150-155, 159.*

Michael Rougier: p. 20 (top)

CONTENTS

ACKNOWLEDGMENTS

6

Any exhibition that focuses on the work of one company in order to illuminate an area of artistic concern inevitably depends on the close cooperation of that company. Fortunately, the basic foundation of Gemini G.E.L. is American free enterprise, with all the practical functions that such industry implies. Without the considerable documentation, both written and photographic, available in Gemini's Los Angeles workshop, it would have been infinitely more difficult to explain the various aspects of Gemini's operation. Conversely, such information made it possible to explore the subject underlying the exhibition by showing works issued by only one company.

The Museum has exhibited in the past lithographs from Universal Limited Art Editions (1964) and Tamarind Lithography Workshop (1969). I am indebted, as is the Director of Gemini G.E.L., to the two women responsible for these workshops, Mrs. Tatyana Grosman and Miss June Wayne, for the dynamic direction they have given printmaking in this country. Without them American artists would still be making prints in college workshops or in Europe. Kenneth Tyler and his wife Kay continued on the path they explored.

With his partners, Sidney Felsen and Stanley Grinstein, Tyler brought to Gemini many of the artists most capable of expanding the concept of what multiple works of art should be. Once there, the artist is exposed to the intense and energetic activity of Tyler and his assistants. The interaction that results from such stimulation is attributable to the very foundation of Gemini—research, development and collaboration.

The exhibition is a selection from almost three hundred works produced by Gemini during the five years of its existence. In attempting to represent the most innovative and momentous projects, I have had to exclude many

worthy of equal attention. Some works for which production time had not been scheduled were rushed to completion for this exhibition. I am most grateful to the directors and staff of Gemini G.E.L. for their accomplishment of this undertaking.

Without the benefit of the previous workshop exhibitions and the continuing inspiration of their director, William S. Lieberman, the Museum's Director of Painting and Sculpture, it would have been impossible even to have attempted this exhibition. Both he and Wilder Green, Director of Exhibitions, were responsible for suggesting that works from Gemini be shown at the Museum, and both deserve my deepest appreciation. Among the many members of the Museum's staff who have been of invaluable assistance are Donna Stein, Assistant Curator in the Department of Prints and Illustrated Books, Richard Palmer, Assistant Director of Exhibitions, and Helen Franc, Editor-in-Chief, whose mine of words and style brought forth the title of the exhibition.

This catalogue exists because of the tenacity and energy of many people both at the Museum and at Gemini. Because all cannot be named here, my particular thanks go to Sandra Fisher at Gemini and the most patient and imaginative editor, Jane Fluegel, at the Museum.

Two artists represented in the exhibition have also contributed a large share to the sum total of it: Jasper Johns, whose multiple acts as a frontispiece to this catalogue, and Roy Lichtenstein, whose *Modern Print* was created for the Museum. Both they and Claes Oldenburg very generously shared with me their memories of working at Gemini.

Finally, my thanks to Ken Tyler, craftsman, collaborator and businessman, who has managed the unusual feat of balancing art and business to the benefit of both.

R.C.   March 1971

TECHNICS AND CREATIVITY

BY RIVA CASTLEMAN

An early 16th-century
printing press, woodcut by
Jodocus Badius

8

While art is basically the product of a creative concept
and the skillful manipulation of materials, only recently
has there begun to be a reaction against the imbalance
that has favored the idea over the means. Technics are
the learned skills, the practical ways of doing something,
the manner and means by which art is accomplished.
An early characterization of man is that of a tool-bearing,
creative animal (whether the tool was meant to scratch
on a wall or kill is an argument best left to anthro-
pologists and sociologists). Fulfilling a creative impulse
with that tool was primitive technics.[1] Once the primary
tool no longer sufficed to complete the act, or the act
itself was divided into a series of processes, it became
correspondingly more difficult for the creator to control
the result. This drastic simplification of the complex
beginnings of technology may explain how the position
of an artist evolved. Although he utilized an increasing
variety of materials and skills — bronze-casting, tapestry-
weaving — in time he could no longer perform independently and became detached from the technological
mainstream. The balance between creativity and technics
shifted.

From the cave man's rudimentary scratching of animal
forms to the Renaissance artist's frescoes, man created
in an environment increasingly demanding of skill and
knowledge. Until the appearance of the printing press,
man could not only assimilate most of the knowledge in
his field but also build upon it. Creative man had only
the burdens of acquiring materials, skilled helpers, and
funds in order to realize his project. If he was exceptionally gifted he would produce works in many fields.
Most importantly, the language necessary to explain the
project to apprentices or patrons was comprehensible.
Neither machines nor materials had developed beyond
the capacities of those who wished to utilize them. This
is not to say that all artists could become engineers or
architects, but that the specialized language of their
technology was understandable to those who wished
to utilize it.

The printing press changed this situation and that of the
artist in the modern world. Once specialized information
could be widely distributed, a gap between creator and
technician developed. Of course, there were many more
"arts" to which man could apply his creative abilities,
but from the point of technics, the "fine" artist began to
stagnate. Until the nineteenth century, the technology of

painting, sculpture, and printmaking grew minutely. Even
with the subsequent introduction of acrylics in painting,
acetylene torches and steel in sculpture, and chemical
processes in printmaking, the comparison with the ratio
of growth in other forms of creative communication is
shattering.

If the machines and materials of art have progressed so
little, attitudes have changed even less. The exhibition
The Machine as Seen at the End of the Mechanical Age[2]
in 1968–69 illustrated the artistic reactions to the tech-
nocracy that emerged in the twentieth century. Previous
Rousseauan attempts to return to nature or ignore the
machine were replaced by amused or horrified renderings
of the machines themselves or the social problems
connected with their advent. Eventually, some of the
forms of technology became the forms of art, particularly
with the appearance of the ready-mades of Marcel
Duchamp. This confrontation with the reality of new form
may ultimately be as influential as man's first look in the
mirror. After a passage of slightly over half a century, a
modern technology for art is beginning to evolve.

The artist has an epithetical name: dreamer. Frequently,
he has exemplified man's nostalgia for a world devoid
of machines and the debris accompanying them. Primitive man used his scratchings to recreate the momentary
event of his own time with materials of his time. In the
West, the trend to a distinction between fine and applied
arts perhaps began as the artist moved away from the
technical complexities that confronted him into more
philosophical areas — areas less responsive to the

Marcel Duchamp, *Bicycle Wheel*, 1951
(3rd version, after lost 1913 original)
The Museum of Modern Art,
The Sidney and Harriet Janis Collection

hundred years of industrial man. The forms of *Letatlin*, the flying machine devised by Tatlin, reminiscent of Leonardo da Vinci's practical experiments, must have mystified the common man, who had already lived through a war in which airplanes were an uncomfortable reality. He, nevertheless, had insight when he wrote in 1932, "An artist with experience of a variety of different materials…will inevitably see it as his duty to solve the technical problem with the help of new relationships in the material…he will try to discover a new, complicated form, which in its further development will naturally have to be technically refined in more detail."[3]

The idea of a total aesthetic, art being put to work, found adherents in the Bauhaus. Although the most exciting products of the Bauhaus method were in applied art, and the aesthetic values of functional objects and archi-tecture were reinforced, very little progress was made in reconciling the artist with industrial methods for the production of works that would fulfill spiritual needs. Images became more and more abstract, and natural forms were altered to resemble objects in an industrial environment. In the case of Josef Albers, who taught courses in stained glass, freehand drawing was no longer a necessary artistic skill. Removing specific "chance" operations from the making of art was a formidable step in making art contemporary.

This exhibition of the products of a workshop devoted to the collaboration of creative and technical people grows from two complex roots: the interaction of technics and creativity outlined briefly above and the technological fact of printmaking. Long before Gutenberg, man had a desire to convey ideas through identical visual material. Perhaps the earliest successful instance was cuneiform, wherein the characters were all incised with the same tool, thus creating a uniform set of impressions. Seals signified authority because of their ability always to form the same image. The impressions of seals are, broadly, the first prints. Where this technique of consistently transferring the same image is unknown, people are unaware that two truly identical things can exist.[4] Too, if it is unknown, no sophisticated monetary systems can be established, nor, more basically, can any form of economics exist that depends on, not simply similarity, but exact equality. Much of the history of technology is the history of man's persistence in trying to make perfectly identical objects.

changing lives of his viewers. Once the artist was no longer challenged by having to master his medium, he tended to examine more methodically ideas of form, space, and light. At that point, the artist-craftsman moved into the ambiguous zone of artist-philosopher. Unlike the philosopher's ideas, however, those of the artist had to be shaped into visual form by tools. In the nineteenth and twentieth centuries, the camera and motion-picture film returned the creative artist to his early, primary profession of documentation. Though painters dabbled with these new tools, specialists evolved—artists less controlled by the ideals of the fine arts.

Although throughout the nineteenth century the artist appears to have been relatively oblivious to the fantastic development of technology, he was not entirely blocked off from the technological build-up. An avant-garde developed that reopened visual investigations into the scientific concepts of light and space. Simultaneously, the artist began to feel the human impact of the mechanical evolution. In the twentieth century, the persistence of wars, the degradation of life through the boredom and pollution created by the machine, the pace of communi-cation that quickly made every new idea obsolete, forced him to react.

The Constructivist movement, for example, was fed by Russian revolutionary theories. Vladimir Tatlin attempted to use the elements of industrial technology to construct a new art for a new society. The human element, how-ever, was still the controlling aesthetic factor, and it was a human element unaware of the realities of nearly a

10

At the beginning of printmaking, the hope of the man who designed playing cards printed from woodblocks was that they would appear identical. Until the advent of machine color printing in the nineteenth century, they never did. Even Dürer's religious prints were issued, and undoubtedly performed their special role in the economics of the time, not as wondrous artistic efforts that had the cachet of uniqueness but as evidences of excellent technical skill that could produce identical copies. After all, connoisseurship that honors uniqueness in supposedly identical things is a reaction against technology. Until recently, if what man wrought was inconsistent with his aim of achieving uniformity, it was cast aside, not treasured for its rarity.

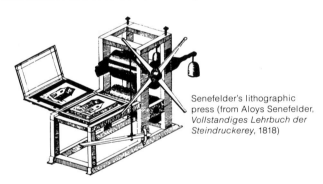

Senefelder's lithographic press (from Aloys Senefelder, *Vollstandiges Lehrbuch der Steindruckerey*, 1818)

With the change in artistic aims after the Renaissance, a more introspective attitude toward prints evolved. The problem-solving attempts—printing variations and retaining them—identify the artist's freedom from the persistent ideal and technological evolution of making identicals. When Senefelder developed lithography in the late eighteenth century, he was fulfilling this ideal, not within the cloistered realm of art but within the continuing technological growth of man. Artists who were not considered printmakers turned to it, but the consistency of lithography must have had a shocking effect on those artists who had previously used for their creative efforts printmaking media that were subject to modification. It was largely ignored until the 1890s, by which time photography had developed and lithography seemed less perfect. However, one important element in lithography forever changed the course of printmaking by artists: the capacity of the stone to print an image consistently (in terms of consistency, the concept of variation

was much broader than today's measurement in millimicrons). The few great artist-printmakers of the past had adopted very personal attitudes toward the way in which the ink was put on the etched or engraved plate. This freedom was denied by lithography.

When in the 1890s artists took up lithography as a medium that could be expanded, it was perhaps in subconscious recognition that they were again participating in the true flow of technology. They relied on printers not only to print but to etch the stone. The possible quantities were so great that the prints became, again, modes of communication, but now with images recognizably by this or that artist. Posters by Lautrec were collectible not for any unique values of the sheets but for the image, and they heralded the return of prints to the realm of true mass media. The counter-reaction was swift in appearing. In the first decades of the twentieth century, the major artists made prints, but few of them were lithographs. The woodcut became for the Germans the most free form of printerly expression, completely inconsistent, and at its best when it emulated the primitive. In the 1930s, Stanley William Hayter developed intaglio techniques to unforeseen heights and fostered a new group of artist-craftsmen, both in Europe and America. Hayter's work so complicated the etching and engraving processes that subtle differences were, of necessity, apparent in the editions.

Lithography in the meantime was consistently used for commercial and art printing in ever-practical America. Until after World War II, when Hayter's students began to appear, art schools were more likely to teach lithography than any other printmaking technique. One of the most typical of the museum-connected art schools, The Art Institute of Chicago, was the starting point in 1950 for Kenneth Tyler, who was to found the Gemini workshop fifteen years later. Tyler learned the techniques of lithography from Max Kahn and found inspiration in the Institute's excellent print collection. Still interested in pursuing his own artistic career, he left Chicago and went on to the Herron School of Art in Indianapolis. By 1963, he was an adept printer with a more than peripheral interest in machinery, possibly developed during his work in Indiana steel mills. He received one of the Ford-Foundation–funded Tamarind Lithography Workshop printer grants, which made it possible for him to become the shop's technical director, after some expert tutelage from Garo Antreasian and the French master printer, Marcel Durassier.

Dan Freeman, printer, printing
Ellsworth Kelly's *Blue/Green*
Gemini, 1970

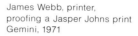

James Webb, printer,
proofing a Jasper Johns print
Gemini, 1971

The Tamarind Workshop was founded by the indomitable June Wayne, who directed it from 1960 to 1970; her goal in this enterprise was twofold: the training of printers in America to guarantee the establishment and continuity of lithography workshops, and the introduction of artists to the medium so that they also would be interested in the continuation of lithography. This idea was inspired by the postwar revival of lithography in France, where such artists as Picasso worked in lithography houses— Mourlot and others. Tamarind, however, was not mere revivalism (its program continues under the aegis of the Ford Foundation at the University of New Mexico) but introduced elements of American "know-how" to a printing craft that had never entirely overcome the bias against its commercial start. Understanding that a medium expands only by the quality of the demands made of it, Miss Wayne worked with a dozen artists each year to uproot the solidified concepts of what could be done with lithography. Her program also researched inks and papers to create a standard that would make the printed product of Tamarind uniform in, at least, manufactured quality. Tyler worked on the research programs that developed a ball-grained aluminum plate which was close in quality to the grain of a stone and could be used in conjunction with stone lithography. Aluminum-plate lithography, particularly as it developed out of this program, has played an important part in the techno-logical advance made in printmaking.

Early in 1965, Tyler and his wife started to print in their garage, and in July they founded Gemini Ltd. With another former Tamarind printer, Bernard Bleha, they set up a shop behind the Los Angeles framing and art-shipping concern, Art Services. While still technical director of Tamarind, Tyler had printed several lithographs for Nicholas Krushenick, and Gemini's first commission, from the Los Angeles County Museum Council, was for a print by this artist to be sold for fund raising. July 1965 was also the moment of the riots in the Watts section of Los Angeles, and the newly designed press was awaiting pick-up there. The ancient ceremony of carrying the fire to a new home was given a modern emulation by the police-protected procession of the lithographic press from Watts to the Gemini workshop.

Timothy Huchthausen,
printer, processing an
Ellsworth Kelly aluminum plate
Gemini, 1970

Stuart Henderson and Ron
McPherson, printers, checking level
of stone with a straight-edge
Gemini, 1969

12

Kenneth Tyler
etching a Frank Stella stone
Gemini, 1971

For a short period Gemini did custom work: for example, a suite by the British Pop artist David Hockney, Giacometti's last lithograph, as well as printing and publishing a book of poetry by Robert Creeley with ten lithographs by the late California artist John Altoon. Eager to put into practice some ideas he had developed over ten years, particularly in expanding the dimension of both the medium and its product, Tyler formed a corporation with two collectors of contemporary art: Sidney B. Felsen, the owner of an accounting firm, and Stanley Grinstein, a manufacturer. The new Gemini G.E.L. (Graphics Editions Limited) now had the capital to commission works, and the first artist to be asked to do a series of prints was Josef Albers. There were many factors that, in retrospect, seem to have made this choice an inspired one. Foremost, Albers' role in transforming art from a hand to a machine orientation immediately activated a new pattern of production. His work necessitated an industrial exactitude rarely demanded of artist-craftsman enterprises. Certain built-in problems of printing—elusive color and paper stretch—had to be controlled if the straight lines and perfect color rhythms of Albers' compositions were to be in harmony. Tyler had already faced these problems at Tamarind with Albers, and now that the editions were to be his own he was challenged to uncover the technology that would perfect this area of printmaking. It took nine months to fix the colors and compositions, another eight to print the sixteen White Line Squares (*VIII* and *XV,* pages 32 and 33).

Before reviewing the work issuing from Gemini, the problems inherent in the technique of lithography should be examined, particularly as to the way they affected Tyler's objectives. Once Tyler was in agreement with the idea that great prints are made by great artists (the subject of a lecture he heard William S. Lieberman give at the University of Southern California in 1964), he realized that the scale of prints had to be closer to the scale of painting being done by the most successful contemporary American artists. In order to make larger prints, the presses had to be not only larger but more precisely balanced; registration had to be more exact; paper had to be made in larger sizes with less elasticity; stones had to be made lighter; and changes had to be made to lessen the strain of printing on the printers themselves. This last point cannot be underestimated. In order to open the door to true collaboration between the artist and technician, the technician would have to undergo an education enabling him to communicate; but if his formative years had been spent in pursuits more akin to the creative life than the active, more than

likely he would be physically incapable of carrying out the tasks that have customarily accompanied stone lithography (a stone 35 inches high x 50 inches wide x 3 inches deep weighs 350 pounds). Whereas the traditional apprentice system created artisans who were both strong and extremely sensitive to their product, the protracted length of American education has almost eradicated long-term training of this type. In the case of Gemini, printer trainees are chosen for their intelligence, mental and physical agility, innate understanding of quality control and identicalness, ambition, and, as much as possible, an unromantic attitude about art and artists. Rather than insisting that the artisans be cogs in an established machine, the machine must be altered to allow them to operate freely, whatever their physique.

Tyler had worked on the idea of a hydraulically operated press while a student in Chicago. A not completely operative version was built in Indianapolis, and finally a press was built in Los Angeles which incorporated a hydraulic cylinder to engage the scraper bar against the stone and a motor to pull the bed back and forth. Subsequent presses have been larger and their machinery more refined. In consultation with engineers and specialists in fields relating to printing, larger presses requiring little manual operation, gauged to the physical type of the person printing, and capable of making impressions from the uniformly stable materials are being developed.

13

Despite the enthusiasm brought to the development of machinery capable of printing large lithographs, further problems emerged in other areas. In order to produce the first large print, Robert Rauschenberg's *Booster* (page 47), in 1967, paper six feet long had to be found. Perhaps if the long-accepted Rives BFK or Arches rag paper had been found in the size needed, another of the research and development programs at Gemini would never have occurred. As it happened, only one type of paper for *Booster* was available, on custom order, and although it had enough stability and durability, it lacked the modulated surface that made most lithographs on Rives and Arches appear more sensitively printed. With the aid of a grant from the National Endowment for the Arts, Gemini began consultation with paper mills in America, France, and Germany primarily to do research on the properties of art paper in order to develop an alkaline pulp paper that would have all the desirable qualities of scarce and expensive rag paper. The undefined aim of the program was to encourage the production of this type of paper in the United States at a cost that would make it available to students. Two problems arose that vividly illuminate the differences between craft and industry. In the family-run paper mill of Arjomari at Epinal, France, secrecy and tradition tended to color both the information about the product and the possibilities for change. Needing very large paper, Gemini hoped to have it produced in rolls. Yet, maintaining the tradition of handmade and mold-made sheets of paper, the managers of the old mill refused for a long time to admit that they were actually producing rolls and cutting them up. American industrial systems provided a second problem. Research in industrial laboratories, once it becomes product-oriented, is usually directed toward making many tons or millions of pieces. To ask the S. D. Warren Company, the developer of excellent book paper, to work on a properly balanced art paper of which possibly only a few tons would be used in a year was one of the first of many audacious confrontations. Terminology mutually understood by artisan and technician had to be agreed upon. The sensitive surface, weight, and flexibility of that ideal paper for lithography required a descriptive phrase, which eventually evolved into "friendly feel."

Essential to all the research, documented in the report on the National Endowment grant, was the presence of a paper expert, Larry Hardy of the Crown Zellerbach Corporation. He was able to interpret Gemini's needs to the paper companies in America and thus discover which of them could actually produce the required type of paper with their facilities. He discovered, too, an inability to communicate with industry when dealing with material that would not produce a high return. Those companies making paper with the necessary permanence (healthy chemical structure) and good printing surface were unable to capture the element of "friendly feel," although they undoubtedly could identify it in other papers. After trial runs at the Rochester Paper Company, it was concluded that only considerable quantities of money could assure the development of the desired paper (one ton of blended rag-pulp alkaline paper was eventually produced by Rochester for Gemini). Certainly, Gemini learned a lesson: once you had a provocative idea, you could enter industrial territory; you could even learn its specialized language and enable it to be responsive to yours; you could encourage research toward your goal and the full force of that industry could be persuaded to use its facilities toward it; but as the economic implications become clearer, the time for research eventually lessens; and as the idea takes physical form, nuances increase and communications diminish.

It is likely that the paper mills questioned during the program were made aware of this new desire to involve industry in art, not as patrons but as collaborators. Experiments in Art and Technology (E.A.T.) and the Los Angeles County Museum's Art and Technology project have attempted to reinforce this involvement. To replace handmade art paper with industrially produced art paper that could have better qualities due to scientific progress is an aim that may have more than an isolated reaction.

Part of the National Endowment grant was to be used for the purpose of developing an embossing method. This was related to the paper program, since the paper used had to be elastic and strong enough to withstand the pressure of embossing and permanently retain the embossed image. It was thought that rather deep embossing could be achieved on the new lithographic press since its pressure could be calibrated almost perfectly. Jasper Johns made his second tour to Gemini in 1969 in order to work on embossed lead reliefs. After attempting to emboss them on the lithographic presses, he discovered that the depth of the relief and the fragility of lead, which had to be reinforced by a rigid backing formed in the same manner, required a uniform pressure applied vertically (stamping), rather than laterally (on the lithographic press the lead was forced out one end of the mold). Male and female molds were made from Johns's wax reliefs, and a hydraulic forming press stamped out each piece.

Josef Albers and Kenneth Tyler
discussing Embossed Linear Construction print
New Haven, Connecticut, 1969

Printers moving
Robert Rauschenberg's
stone, *Waves,* onto press bed
Gemini, 1969

16   The forming press was also used for Josef Albers'
Embossed Linear Constructions in 1969, but since the
depth of the relief was quite small, male and female
molds were not required. What was needed, however,
was accurate engraving of the plate. As noted before,
Albers insisted on mechanical perfection rather than
human imperfection for his images. In order to obtain it,
a programmer reduced the drawings to digital tape
which electronically activated an automatic engraving
mill to incise the mirror image of the drawing onto an
aluminum plate. The variable was the profile of the line
to be engraved; both Tyler and the programmer drafted
contours for the milling head of the engraver, and the
artist approved the resulting line he preferred.

Josef Albers' relationship with Gemini (he has never
visited the workshop, much less worked there) is akin to
a designer's relationship with the factory producing his
design. Other artists have preferred to set up close
working relationships with the printers in the now more
or less classical stance taken by Picasso in the late
1940s. They use the shop as an extension of their studio,

building and embellishing their compositions as proofs
are run. In this process there is much interaction, with
the technically adept printer offering suggestions on how
this or that technique might enhance the image, how a
paper or ink might solve certain problems. This element
of collaboration is always present at Gemini, to a greater
degree with artists who develop their composition on
the stone and plate, rather than with those who merely
add elements to their initial image. Foremost among
those in the first category is Robert Rauschenberg. His
Booster and the seven studies for it challenged the workshop in 1967, for all at once the printers were working
with an artist so familiar with lithographic techniques
that he could require of them the exercise of their entire
range of skills and demand that they find new solutions.
His use of photographic materials such as X-rays and
newspaper half-tones, as well as other mechanically produced elements, recalls the work of Schwitters, who was
among those artists in the 1920s who had participated
in the earliest confrontation with mechanical materials.

Rauschenberg, before he was introduced to lithography,
had made blueprints and a long print from an automobile
tire run through ink. His lithographs printed at Universal
Limited Art Editions (ULAE) from 1962 until 1966 used
zinc cuts and mats from newspapers to transfer photographic images to the stones. *Booster's* photographic elements were transfers from photolithographic plates, and
the linear astronomical charts were silkscreened over the
lithograph.

The inevitable confusion between process and creativity
is most obviously called to mind by Rauschenberg's
work, standing as it does on the threshhold between
gesture and machine translation. In the promotional
brochure *Booster and 7 Studies,* Lucy Lippard writes,
"Even the colors are objects in themselves—conte, sepia,
red pencil, blueprint—easily identifiable as casual facts
of execution rather than acts of creation."[5] Max Kozloff,
after referring to *Booster,* writes, "The more he can
demonstrate his own bodily processes to be like those
of a machine, the more incisive his rhetoric: the demolition
of a merely personal artistic choice."[6] These statements
insinuate that the ascendancy of the technical or mechanical diminishes the personal creative act. A confrontation
with an X-ray of Rauschenberg is no less of an aesthetic
experience than one with a thirteenth-century madonna.
Both are suppositions of reality.

George Page and Ron Adams, printers,
printing Josef Albers' *White Embossing on Gray I*
Amsco, Los Angeles, 1970

Robert Rauschenberg drawing
on stones during Stoned Moon project
Gemini, 1969

If the technician is a cog in the wheel of Rauschenberg's technique, he is the source of energy in Lichtenstein's. Rauschenberg takes the results of machine production and combines it, partly mechanically, with his own brush-work. Lichtenstein takes the mechanical means of translating form (the dots of a half-tone screen) and subjugates it to his personal framework. His series of Cathedrals (*Cathedral #5,* page 41) and Haystacks from 1969 capture a spectrum of color changes similar to those of Monet, but he uses the contemporary means to which our eyes have become accustomed. Monet's jabs of color resulted in diffused forms that might have been viewed through rain-spattered glass or by a myopic eye. Lichtenstein's series is dependent on a code of dots our brains are now prepared to translate into form. The mechanical methods for adaptation of shape and shade are now

viable tools for the artist. Since these designs are pre-determined in photographic reproduction, there is no reason why they cannot be part of the process of art and therefore applied by a technician. Lithographs by Lichtenstein are made from aluminum plates with stencils, hand-cut by the Gemini printers. He presents his com-positions in final form and is attentive to the proofing, realigning shapes and changing colors throughout the printing process, but only through consultation. His artistic motions could easily be exchanged with those of an industrial designer, if his intent were to create a functional design rather than an interpretive work. Lichtenstein's transformation of known art objects through an almost unalterable set of forms could be considered the visual equivalent of twelve-tone music. As Frederic Tuten writes of this group of Lichtenstein's: "In the Monet painting and prints, the dot and all the inflections and nuances of the dot, is its own subject, not merely a vehicle for image-making."[7]

The serial nature of Lichtenstein's Cathedrals and Hay-stacks is a basis for Frank Stella's work at Gemini, as well. Like Albers and Rauschenberg, he chose to produce a unified group of lithographs, and it was his first experience with the medium. His first attempts were the Black series, related to the group of paintings done between 1959 and 1960. Like Jasper Johns, whose early flat paintings had influenced him, Stella also chose to dip into his past work for his print imagery. Having to sacrifice the insistent edge of the canvas (vital to the containment of his radiating lines) to the white field of paper, he chose to place his forms off center and make of the series a sort of notebook. Removing the Black series from the linear readability of his large paintings in exhibition, he made his first attempt to come to terms with the obvious necessity to alter the dimension of his work. The paper in both the Black and later Aluminum and Copper series acts as the proper environment for the image, containing it and inducing a one-to-one impact equal to that of Stella's insistently symmetrical paintings. Once Stella set out to work on a larger scale, he seems to have sought some way to reconcile the intimacy of paper with the character of his forms that might allow the print to be displayed on a wall. The Star of Persia group (page 52) was printed on graph paper, enclosing the symmetrical form in an area which might have structured it. The Stars (done in 1967) recall paintings of 1963-64, and lay bands of flat, glossy color on a grid in quite the manner of his drawings. The use of a mechanical surface and ink that lives on the surface

dependent on

19

rather than becoming one with it resulted in new technical problems. Inks were developed that would have the metallic sheen of the paint he was using. The shapes in the V series of 1968 (page 53) are related to the paintings of 1964-65. Robert Rosenblum writes: "The wedge-shaped canvas, with its swift ascent of convergent (or descent of divergent) strips, is almost a twentieth-century symbol for abstract, mechanized speed . . . And even the icy colors . . . conform to this mechanized imagery that provides, as it were, an abstract counterpart to the more explicit use of industrial reproductive techniques (Ben-Day dots, commercial paints, stencils) in much Pop art of the mid-1960's."[8] Stella's use of unaltered commercial paints was, however, as provocative a use of technologically produced material as Lichtenstein's sheet of dots. Translating this into lithography led to the development of new inks and papers, feeding back into the field of printing further exploitable, industrially produced goods.

Equating the artist's demands with the time and need for technical innovation should also be considered in terms of economics. Although research on paper may have direct rewards for both Gemini's printing of lithographs and the art student, perhaps this is not a large enough reward for industry. Until the possible return to industry can be envisioned in dollars, development of materials oriented toward the arts is slow and subject to much experimentation. The most extreme case of development of material and techniques experienced by Gemini was in the production of Claes Oldenburg's *Profile Airflow* (page 57). The concept of this work was not unique in Oldenburg's oeuvre. In 1966, he had created for Multiples, Inc. (New York) a *Tea Bag,* made up of elements including a silkscreened felt bag, encased in vacuum-formed clear vinyl. For the *Airflow,* which is also a molded clear plastic surface over a printed image, Oldenburg wished to use color and have the plastic slightly soft to the touch. The imperfections of the vinyl *Tea Bag* had to be eliminated in order to "read" the *Airflow:* plastic soft enough to have the tactile quality Oldenburg sought was not rigid enough to maintain the proper surface—or if rigid, it was not clear. Oldenburg himself spent a year working on the wood model from which a mold would be made. The roster of specialists who participated in the experiments to develop the perfect process for accomplishing the plastic shell included the elite of the Southern California plastics industry. The Chrysler Airflow was designed by Carl Breer (father of Oldenburg's friend, the artist Robert Breer)

and first produced in 1934. Polyurethane, the plastic finally used for Oldenburg's piece, was introduced into the United States twenty years later, and fifteen years after that the multiple ("object print" is the Gemini term) appeared. During the gestation of Oldenburg's piece, specialists who could relate to an art project did not have enough knowledge to solve the problems. In his report to the National Foundation on the Arts and the Humanities, whose Endowment grant enabled him to explore a "Three-Dimensional Graphic Program," Tyler writes, "Finding a technician that could identify to an art project, and who had the physical resources and ability to communicate on a specific level in plastics was a major task. In a hand craft one must become involved with people in the making stages before they can reveal their degree of efficiency and technological know-how. Finding the right facility and person was very difficult. . . . The major reasons for this were lack of substantial funds to promise industry handsome profits, and the lack of time to wait for available production time from an industry that scheduled twelve to eighteen months ahead."[9] In fact, Gemini soon found that a member of the industrial complex who had his own laboratory was the only possible help. Oriented toward research, he was able to enter into the project as an experimental exercise. Because the field of plastics is one of the most recently developed, it is made up of specialists, and even the plastics engineer needed the aid of other engineers and resin specialists. In the exceptional article introducing the *Airflow,* Barbara Rose writes: "If the *Airflow* multiple proves one thing, however, it is this: no artist of Oldenburg's calibre and powerful originality has anything to worry about in the 'dehumanizing' or 'depersonalizing' aspects of technology. The unpredictable visual impact of the *Airflow* . . . reveals that the contemporary artist can master technology as his ancestors conquered nature, although probably with as much effort."[10] A basic fact that brings us up short in the study of this further monument to man's dependence on the beloved object is that it, like its model, was a financial disaster,[11] cost its eventual owners more than twice the cost of the Chrysler model, and had to be "called back" in the finest of Detroit traditions, since the current amount of air pollution in America made the sea-blue polyurethane shell discolor. A colored plastic with a life of a thousand years has been developed to replace the old model!

Claes Oldenburg sanding
wood model for *Profile Airflow*
Gemini, 1968

It is possible that the techniques and materials developed for the *Airflow* will have repercussions in industry. The imagination and courage of artists are what will place them in the mainstream of technological development, and Claes Oldenburg seems to engender ideas and solutions that force the issue of true collaboration. Oldenburg's *Ice Bag,* which Gemini executed in an eighteen-foot version under the Los Angeles County Museum's Art and Technology program and showed in Expo '70 at Osaka, is recorded in a film that upgrades the visual nature of what is essentially an educational message. The ideas that led to the creation of *Ice Bag* are outlined in the movie, *Sort of a Commercial for an Ice Bag* (page 61), directed by Michel Hugo. The virtuosity of the artist, who spent only one day being filmed, is captured in the gestures of his freehand drawing, while the imaginative inspiration of the diverse materials offered to the spectator expand the experience of the final construction.

Unlike many of the artists who come to Gemini either with projects in mind or completely drawn up, Oldenburg prefers to look for his inspiration and materials in or around the neighborhood of the workshop. Whereas Tyler often anticipates the material requirements of his artists, and occasionally will rush a project forward in order to retain the momentum brought to it by the artist, much of the work with Oldenburg does not take place in the workshop. During the making of

Ice Bag—Scale A during construction
Krofft Enterprises, North Hollywood, 1969

the Osaka *Ice Bag,* conference telephone calls often sufficed for many of the decisions. Oldenburg recognizes that his technological requirements, while still more complex than those needed by most artists, generally call for pre-World-War-II techniques. He believes that scientists involved in art and technology programs tend to be too theoretical, and he must work with tangibles. By being in touch with the makers of things, he experiences a feedback into his own work.

The *Ice Bag* itself, also made as a multiple in four- and twelve-foot (page 60) versions, is a fantasy subjected to a severe case of *gigantis extremis.* It is, so far, the only kinetic multiple produced by Gemini and the first created by Oldenburg (discounting the movie, of course). What it accomplishes through movement, reflection of light, transformation of shape, and modulation of sound is both a parody and exaltation of the earliest machines. Divorced from its utility, the *Ice Bag* confronts us with a provocative reference to modern life. Each version is also a triumph of mechanical engineering. The largest *Ice Bag,* for example, "measures 18 feet in diameter at the base and slowly moves from 7 feet rest height to a maximum of 16 feet while performing its 'twisting, rotating like motion.' The piece has an electronic speed control motor (1 through 30 rpm) to produce swivel action of the bag. A two to one reduction rotor chain sprocket system causes the hydraulic unit to rotate the bag (1½ rpm). Pressure is 600 psi for running hydraulic cylinders at a thrust force of 8,000 pounds. System operates with a hydraulic pump (capacity 25 gallons). Main hydraulic system has 4 inch pistons with a five foot stroke. Rods are 2½ inches in diameter. . . ."[12]

If the *Ice Bag* refers obliquely to the uncomfortable ramifications of existence in the middle of the twentieth century, Lichtenstein provides us with allusions to the bleak 1930s in his Peace Through Chemistry prints (page 43) and bronze (page 42). In 1934, Lewis Mumford insisted, "We cannot intelligently accept the practical benefits of the machine without accepting its moral imperatives and its aesthetic forms."[13] The need to strengthen the Depression-damaged moral fiber of man by allying him with the underlying cause of his betrayal gave a frantic determination to the so-called *art moderne* of the period. Lichtenstein transforms this spiritual charade into patterns that convey the forms of modernity through the materials basic to their accomplishment. The *Peace Through Chemistry Bronze,* with the commercial patina of cemetery monuments, con-

founds the problem of means and ends. Produced in a foundry simultaneously turning out commemorative plaques for Disneyland, Lichtenstein's bronze takes on the character of an *objet trouvé,* credible only in our own time.

A capital moment of our time in which history and event occurred simultaneously was man's visit to the moon. Robert Rauschenberg was one of the artists chosen by the National Aeronautics and Space Administration (NASA) to commemorate this triumph. Having long allied himself with the news media through his plundering of its visual content as well as his own contributions to *Time* and *Life* magazines, Rauschenberg was able to recognize and select meaningful material from an original source. NASA. The thirty-three lithographs result from the artist's direct experience with the mammoth enterprise, as a spectator with eyes attuned to remarking the unusual as well as the almost invisible ordinary. The scale of machinery, the candy-sweet color bleached by the Florida sun, the pace of human and mechanical activity, the enigma of bird and rocket, all fall beneath his perspicacious eye and are rendered as stroboscopic images of the total event. In an earlier series of lithographs, *Reels (B + C),* Rauschenberg made use of a mechanical event, the movie *Bonnie and Clyde,* to recapitulate visual materials. The film was already an art form, vividly recalled by many for the subtle colors of the photography, Rauschenberg sought to evoke an additional dimension in his interpretation by using fluorescent colors in his lithographs. The Stoned Moon series is a tour de force of compelling and mystifying images, whirled into new identities by a creative force. In their imaginative and complete use of the lithographic process, including photo-sensitive stones, offset lithography, embossing, reversing the image chemically, and the methods Rauschenberg had developed over the years to the point of being traditional, the Stoned Moon prints may be Rauschenberg's most complete statement in the medium. The printers at the Gemini workshop worked as a team with the artist, and the weeks and months necessary for the proofing of each composition were spent in teamlike solidarity, living each minute for the project. It is no wonder that Rauschenberg was relieved to turn to a silkscreen project made from his own collages *(Currents),* which he could accomplish, for the most part, alone.

22

Roy Lichtenstein drawing on
Peace Through Chemistry I aluminum plate
Gemini, 1969

Hand chasing
Peace Through Chemistry Bronze
Classic Bronze, El Monte, 1969

What was the Gemini involvement during this moon-shot project? The shop worked on it for almost a year (the launch was in July 1969; the last editions were completed in July 1970). During that time *Sky Garden* (page 49) and *Waves* were printed (at eighty-nine inches high, they are the largest hand-pulled lithographs ever made). From *Booster* to *Sky Garden,* Tyler's conviction that prints must attain greater dimension to be meaningful seems to have provoked images that would determine extreme sizes.

With *Sky Garden,* Tyler believes that, at least in a vertical format, he has accomplished his aim. The recitation of the progression of work on the entire series reveals the pressure under which the shop operated. Four stones cracked, and three compositions had to be printed with stones in progressively deteriorating states (programs for the conservation of lithographic limestone, one of which was initiated by June Wayne, predict the demise of this material in the near future). The paper program had finally produced results in France, and Gemini had in hand large rolls of Arjomari paper that would impart to *Sky Garden* what had been admittedly lacking in *Booster,* a surface compatible with the material impressed upon it. Inks of considerable variety, the products of unending research, were used in the series—silver, gloss varnish, transparent tan and green—and all were developed to be compatible with the paper.

While still at Tamarind, Tyler had been doing research in inks. He was to find that most inks were produced in a semi-finished state, generally for offset printing. The so-called raw ink was in reality processed to a certain consistency before it was distributed and could be modified only slightly. While the research at Tamarind had led basically to the development of permanent colors in consistently performing inks, Tyler found that the raw materials were becoming either unavailable or obsolete. One other development that was useful, particularly in the printing of the large works, was originated for the Stella V prints. In Stella's work, the registration had to be so carefully measured that the paper was hooked to a movable bar. (Each color is printed from a separate plate or stone, therefore perfect placement or registration is necessary.) This device, familiar enough in commercial printing, became practical once Gemini cut its paper from rolls and could punch one end of the sheet and later cut it off after all colors

had been printed. Registration, the most nervewracking part of printing, became with this simple combination of device and modified material the open sesame to large color prints, such as *Sky Garden.*

Another device culled from the more commercial world was a split fountain from an offset press, dismantled and reinstalled in the form of four rollers oscillating a larger roller. This rather Rube Goldbergian machine was the means of inking the thirty-inch-long, ten-inches-in-diameter roller used to ink Jasper Johns's Color Numerals (pages 35-37). For smaller prints, Johns had found that rolling through colored inks on a palette would give him the spectrum or *ombré* effect he desired. The Numerals to be printed in color were much larger in size so that the normal roller would not have been able to ink the stone in one full turn. Once the roller was made large enough (several were manufactured before a perfect one appeared), one man could not ink it. The inking fountain was devised, ink was hand-fed into it, the rollers oscillated, blending the inks slightly, and the large roller was dropped in. It took six months for the ten Color Numerals, printed first in the colored spectrum and then in white, to be printed in an edition of seventy. Johns, a marvelous draftsman and consummate lithographer, seems perhaps the most conservative in the Gemini group of the past five years. He uses crayon and tusche, an occasional transfer for its appearance more than its content, and rarely exacts a technological innovation. He is, nevertheless, the most demanding of printmakers. The Gemini printer can never bask in the glory of technological triumphs if he cannot also master the art of etching a Johns stone and printing it. Johns's work may not press the workshop forward into a future lock-up with industry, but it does harness the hand, heart, and mind into creative collaborative activity. He, too, was led into making his largest print, *Gray Alphabets,* at Gemini. The working environment at Gemini was different enough from the workshop of ULAE, where Johns had done all his previous prints, to make him inclined to start from the beginning. This, for Johns, meant returning to serial or sequential subjects, alphabets and numbers. Because of the rapidity with which proofs could be pulled and corrected, the presence of several printers instead of one, the possibility of obtaining needed materials in a matter of

24

minutes instead of days, and, in fact, the size of the workshop, Johns found that he worked differently. This is manifest both in the size of his prints and the appearance of a spontaneity and breadth of brushstroke quite different from his previous work. The Numerals, printed in their first state from one stone and one aluminum plate, are technically a catalogue of the processes of lithography. These are in the main the classic techniques and do not represent new modes of printmaking. In the colored version, another plate was added, printed in white, giving greater definition to the number as well as introducing a few elements, gestural and mechanical, that opened the composition to further interpretation.

As noted earlier, Johns's second project at Gemini was a series of embossed lead reliefs of some of his sculptured themes, including the light bulb (page 39), toothbrush *(The Critic Smiles),* and flag. It was hoped that this embossing could be accomplished by running the molds made from wax reliefs through the lithographic press. Although the lead reliefs were eventually molded in a hydraulic stamping machine, one print, *No* (page 38), was embossed on the press, and incorporates a piece of die-cut lead as well. More than any other of Johns's edition works, *No,* because it incorporates an additional element structurally disengaged and of another material, has a closer affinity to his painted constructions. Rigidly contained within its white margins, the nervous field of crayon lines surrounds the small uncompromising "no" cut out in lead and appearing to flutter at the end of an embossed line that acts as a wire. As always with Johns, the function of words is continually questioned by the setting into which they are introduced; the tenuousness of the plate at the wire's end questions the precision that "no" is thought to express. The light bulb in his lead relief hangs isolated within uninhabited space, unable to perform its function of illuminating, much as *No* lacks the query that would give it function.

Roy Lichtenstein has done all his sculptural work at Gemini in the last few years. He began work on a series of heads in February 1969. For the entirely sculptural ones, he worked on layers of cardboard and made precise drawings. One of the heads was to be made in glass, but although Gemini presented the problem to the major fine-glass manufacturers both in America and France, no one could produce a perfect piece.

The entire series, which echoes Jawlensky's Constructivist Heads, is a conscious abstraction and emphasizes elements that evoke 1930s stylistic motifs. Turning to relief printing (wood and zinc cuts), Lichtenstein composes with cool, mechanical hard lines, as obdurate as the sharp edges of the brass of his sculptures. Even in the *Modern Head Relief* (page 45), in which flat cutouts of brass stand in low relief against a polished plaque, the play of light does not soften the rigidity, and in fact emphasizes the fixedness of every space and line.

The trend at Gemini has been increasingly toward three-dimensional works as the shop's capacity to collaborate with manufacturers of specialized materials expands. Claes Oldenburg was the first to bring the workshop into true confrontation with the production of so-called multiples. Although printmaking in the twentieth century has been conceived of as multiple, with the production of prints expanding to fill a numerical quota, the production of three-dimensional objects in editions has grown faster in Europe than in America. There, of course, sculpture has continued to be cast in limited editions, and printmaking and casting had access to enough hand capability so that reproductions of twentieth-century three-dimensional works could be undertaken (Man Ray and Duchamp) and new works commissioned. In Switzerland, Daniel Spoerri and Karl Gerstner began work on their Multiplication Arts Transformable (MAT) in 1959, issuing a group of fourteen objects in an edition of a hundred. In America, Mrs. Rosa Esman was among the first to produce, through her Tanglewood Editions, multiples by American artists (*7 Objects in a Box* appeared in 1966 and included pieces by Lichtenstein and Oldenburg). Hers was not the first instance of American multiple-making, but the publication had a larger edition (100) than is usual in sculpture and involved several artists. Lichtenstein had previously made enameled metal reliefs, and in 1964 Rauschenberg had produced at ULAE his *Shades,* lithographs on plexiglass plates that could be interchanged within a metal framework. Few of the works had been produced in large editions, and certainly the capabilities of manufacture in the United States were

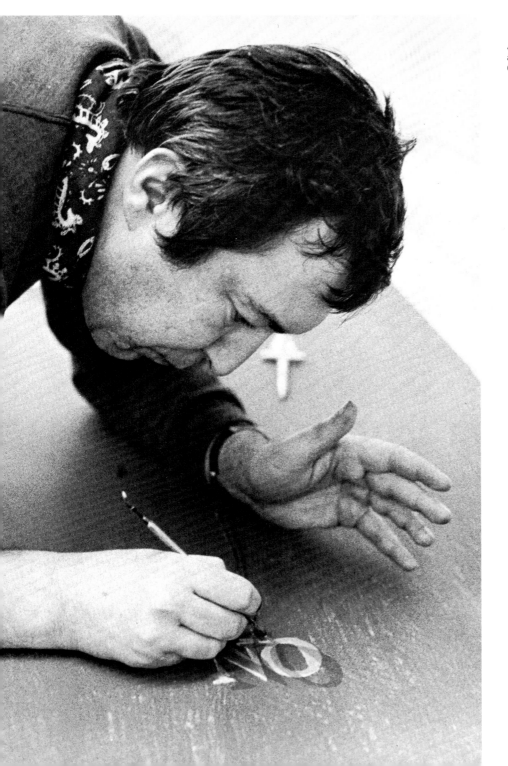

Jasper Johns
affixing lead image to *No*
Gemini, 1968

Jeff Sanders, technician,
spraying synthetic coating on *Le Molé*
Gemini, 1971

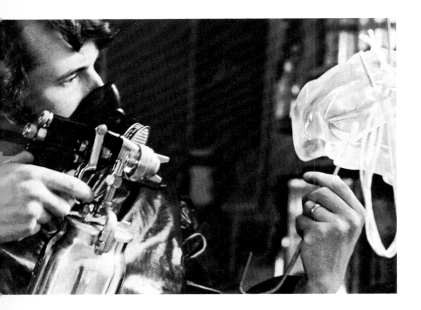

Edward Kienholz
painting urethane on *Sawdy*
Gemini, 1971

inadequate to carry out the complex processes necessary to make multiples in various materials. It was necessary for publishers such as Mrs. Esman or Multiples, Inc. to seek out people who knew how to carry out those processes, or the artist had to search for himself.[14] Production of many multiples has been delayed because publishers or directors of workshops have had to create lines of communication between manufacturers of various materials before elements of the finished work can be finally assembled. Where exceptionally refined processes must be used to finish a sculptured work, the pieces must be moved from factory to factory. In the case of John Chamberlain's *Le Molé* (page 69), for example, the final stop was in the studio of Larry Bell, who had to have for his own work a machine of such sophistication that he bought a U.S. Air Force high-vacuum optical coating machine. There the Chamberlain *Le Molé* was coated with vaporized crystals, emerging with a luminescent sheen reminiscent of both Tiffany glass and the metallic paint used on automobiles in the late 1940s.

Chamberlain, Don Judd, and Edward Kienholz came to Gemini specifically to make three-dimensional works. Kienholz's *Sawdy* (page 68) incorporates a silkscreen in much the same way as certain information on the operation of a machine is indelibly printed on it. The continuing work of other artists simultaneously moves within and expands the capacities of Gemini. Oldenburg, who consciously challenged the printing emphasis of the workshop in 1968 by creating his *Airflow*, hopes to continue with the rest of that project: the taillight, door, and radiator. For these he needs further development in the technology of materials he wants to use, particularly in the casting of rubber. At one time he had hoped to work with a plastic-impregnated corrugated cardboard, but experimentation did not provide a solution at the moment he needed it. Although the process was not fully developed for Oldenburg's project, Rauschenberg later required the same material for his *Cardbird Door* (page 51). This work is made of the ubiquitous torn, unfolded, and reconstructed cartons of our mid-twentieth-century culture. It is, ironically, a multiple assemblage of multiples. Rauschenberg's use of photographic and typographic material for texture, rhythm, and message in his painting and prints is not too different from this collage of squares and rectangles, words, letters, and symbols. The *Cardbird Door* is also a two-sided work that can never be seen all at once. Although concealing its entire form at all times, the *Cardbird Door* is like all doors—one of many.

Oldenburg, in the meantime, has a multitude of mice in the works. Classified by ear size, the multiple mice are in four scales, in addition to one unique mouse with a nine-foot ear. At Gemini he has devised sizes "c" and "d," the former with a nine-inch ear, in black metal (*Geometric Mouse—Scale C,* page 56) and "d" with a six-inch ear, in white. The largest *Geometric Mouse, Variation I,* fabricated by Lippincott Environmental Arts, Inc., in New Haven, Connecticut, was exhibited in the Sculpture Garden of The Museum of Modern Art during Oldenburg's retrospective in 1969.

Gemini has not moved away from printing entirely. With the complex demands of Rauschenberg's Stoned Moon project, the printers found their skills finely honed. Almost simultaneously, Ellsworth Kelly and Frank Stella had ideas for prints that put the emphasis on a different aspect of lithography, the printing of flat and brilliant color. The printers, who had spent the better part of a year making sure that the fine lines in a NASA photograph would not fill in, went back to the cutting of broad shapes in Rubylith. Kelly started working on his series (pages 65 and 66) in April 1969, but no proofing of his prints was done before January 1970. By that time a very white paper had been manufactured to carry the strong flat color that Kelly used for his geometric forms. Whereas in his earlier set of color lithographs, printed in Paris in 1966, he was restricted to a single size of paper, he had many options at Gemini, both in size and in material. John Coplans wrote in August 1970: "In these works Kelly replaces the typical inertness of rectilinear shapes by an active and restless format. These boxlike forms also exploit visual paradox: what is in fact flat takes on the appearance of being dimensional; the eye is played against the mind by inducing 'illusions of illusion' through distortions of geometry."[15] This is all accomplished by the careful juxtaposition of colors that work in a telling degree of opposition to one another. Their vibrancy upon the white paper, equally determining the character of color forms, results from the transparency of the inks used. Like the Albers White Line Square series, Kelly's colors need perfect balance in luminescence and weight of intensity. Until this can be achieved through the use of sophisticated computer techniques, and as long as the printer's materials last, the hands and skills of the artist and printer will be with us.

Ellsworth Kelly cancelling aluminum plate for *Blue/Black* Gemini, 1970

28

Ron Davis, Kenneth Tyler, and
Ron Trnavsky, printer,
comparing proofs of Cube series
Graphic Press, Los Angeles, 1970

Kenneth Price and
Lloyd Venerable, curator,
discussing quality of *Figurine Cup II*
Gemini, 1970

Frank Stella's work has continued to utilize the workshop's skills and facilities, with his running series of Aluminums and Coppers, a group of Stacks, and a large square "protractor" style silkscreen, *Referendum '70*. The latter work led directly into a group of very large, flat, and vividly colored lithographs titled Newfoundland series. *Port aux Basques* (page 55), the largest print in this group, is a stunning interlacing of pastel and dense colors, capturing the delicious exuberance of his very large paintings of 1967-69. Pointing out Hiberno-Saxon and Islamic influences in Stella's paintings of these years, William Rubin writes, "It is not surprising that these styles (as well as Orphic Cubism and 1930s 'moderne') should have been invoked in discussions of his recent work, particularly in connection with the interlace and rainbow pictures . . . Stella himself sees the work of Delaunay as being the most important of these influences. . . ."[16]

Both Ken Price and Ron Davis have worked on prints that have required photo-offset printing. This is a technical direction that Tyler forecast, but with considerable anxiety. Until Gemini could build its own plant to separate the noisy offset machinery and different pace of work from the lithography workshop, he was wary of bringing an artist into direct confrontation with printers who would not comprehend a novel way of working. One of Price's Figurine Cup series was the first to be printed by photo-offset. Since a photographic image was used in the lithographed plates of the series (page 40), some of the Gemini printers could work with the offset people and interpret the artist's needs. Davis wanted the even more rigid system of "process" color separation in his Cubes (page 62). The prints are laminated between sheet Mylar and plastic, and have a glossy, slightly blurring finish covering the variable screen of mixed colors in somewhat sharper definition than his two-dimensional plastic works.

Many aspects of the performance of the workshop have been described under the various artists' projects. Ideally, the printers move with ease from one activity to another, from graining a stone to matching an ink to cutting paper for an edition. This last job is generally done by the curator, who is ultimately responsible for the collating and stamping of a uniform edition. After the artist has signed and numbered the completed prints or multiples, the curator embosses the "chop" of the workshop and the copyright symbol. The curator is also responsible for the care of the completed editions and

performs the perhaps more demanding function of quality control. Beyond the documentation recorded on the worksheets kept by the printer, photographers continually record the activities of the artists in the shop, and critics survey the works in progress.

Few publishers have introduced their products with promotional materials of such high quality. Well-designed brochures with careful reproductions are absolute necessities for a company specializing in fine printing. The essays have been prepared by many of the outstanding writers on contemporary art, several of whom have been quoted here. Their brief statements on series or sets of prints have sometimes been the first isolated descriptions of an artist's printed work. The brochures are not only comparable to critical introductions to books and portfolios but are also further examples of Gemini's contemporary acumen.

Lewis Mumford, for whom the term "technics" has served for decades to spotlight his particular interpretation of man's past and future condition, said in 1951, "Man truly lives only to the extent that he transforms and creates out of the raw materials of life a world whose meaning and values outlast his original experiences and transcends its limitations. . . . For art to perform this function, however, at least one condition is necessary: man must respect his own creativity."[17] The "raw materials of life" no longer consist of stone and nature's colors. Increasingly, the artist will have to be surrounded by those members of the advanced realm of technics who can apply what they and scientists have independently created. One of the ways for this to happen is in the development of small industries where the creation of multiple art works will take precedence over the independent and unique object. Like the third and fourth ready-made *Bicycle Wheel* produced by Duchamp as the demand grew, so multiple art should be as subject to demand as it is to the economics that have so far limited it. The expanding technics of art brings companies such as Gemini G.E.L. to the threshhold of this future responsibility.

NOTES

30

[1]Thomas Munro, *Evolution in the Arts* (Cleveland, Ohio: The Cleveland Museum of Art, 1963), p. 379: "In recent years the word 'technics' has been increasingly used. As distinguished from 'technology,' it means the active skills and processes themselves, whereas the latter word refers more to the knowledge, theory, or science developed in connection with such skills. The chipping of flint is a technic; a particular chipped arrow-head is a technical device; the knowledge of how to chip flints is a kind of primitive technology."

[2]*The Machine as Seen at the End of the Mechanical Age*, New York. The Museum of Modern Art, November 25, 1968-February 9, 1969.

[3]"Art out into Technology," 1932, English translation by Keith Bradfield, in exhibition catalogue, *Vladimir Tatlin* (Stockholm: Moderna Museet, July-September 1968).

[4]Marshall McLuhan, *Understanding Media: The Extensions of Man* (New York: The McGraw-Hill Book Company, 1965), p. 174: "Margaret Mead has reported that when she brought several copies of the same book to a Pacific island there was great excitement. The natives had seen books, but only one copy of each, which they assumed to be unique. Their astonishment at the identical character of several books was a natural response to what is after all the most magical and potent aspect of print and mass production. It involves a principle of extension by homogenization that is the key to understanding Western power."

[5]*Robert Rauschenberg: Booster and 7 Studies* (Los Angeles: Gemini G.E.L., 1967), n.p.

[6] "The Division of Mocking of the Self," *Studio International* (London), vol. 179, no. 918 (January 1970), p. 14.

[7]*Lichtenstein at Gemini* (Los Angeles: Gemini G.E.L., 1969), n.p.

[8]*Frank Stella* (Baltimore: Penguin Books, Inc., 1971), pp. 36, 39.

[9]Kenneth Tyler, "Final Progress Report on Gemini Grant, A-04291-68-1511, February 1969" (unpublished), for National Foundation on the Arts and the Humanities, Washington, D.C.

[10]*Profile Airflow* (Los Angeles: Gemini G.E.L., 1970), n.p.

[11]Quoting from *The Complete Encyclopedia of Motor Cars 1885-1968* (New York: E. P. Dutton and Co., Inc., 1968), edited by G. N. Georgano: "The Chrysler line for 1934 was spearheaded by the revolutionary CU-type 8-cylinder Airflow, with welded unitary construction of chassis and body, all seats within the wheel base, head lamps mounted flush in the wings, a full aerodynamic shape and concealed luggage accommodation. At $1,345 it was a commercial failure, though it was continued till 1937."

[12]"Claes Oldenburg's Ice Bag," *E.A.T.L.A.* [Experiments in Art and Technology, Los Angeles], Survey 2 (February 1970), p. 3.

[13]*Technics and Civilization* (New York: Harcourt, Brace and World, Inc., 1934, Harbinger Book Edition, 1963), p. 355.

[14]Reyner Banham, "Aesthetics of the Yellow Pages," *New Society* (London), vol. 8, no. 203 (1966), p. 271: "The classified telephone directory is the standard guide to the availability of New Cottage Industries, which is why the style that exploits them is sometimes called the yellow pages aesthetic. A glance at the yellow pages will show what a range of specialist Cottage Industries London has."

[15]*Ellsworth Kelly* (Los Angeles: Gemini G.E.L., 1970), n.p.

[16]*Frank Stella* (New York: The Museum of Modern Art, 1970), p. 146.

[17]From the Bampton Lectures delivered at Columbia University in 1951: *Art and Technology* (New York: Columbia University Press, 1952), p. 141.

PLATES

Josef Albers, *White Line Square VIII*, 1966

Josef Albers, *White Line Square XV*, 1966

34

Josef Albers, *White Embossing on Gray I,* 1971

Jasper Johns, *Figure 7*, 1969

Jasper Johns. *Color Numeral Series*, 1969

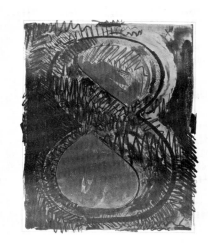

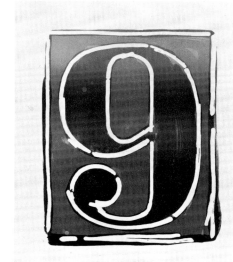

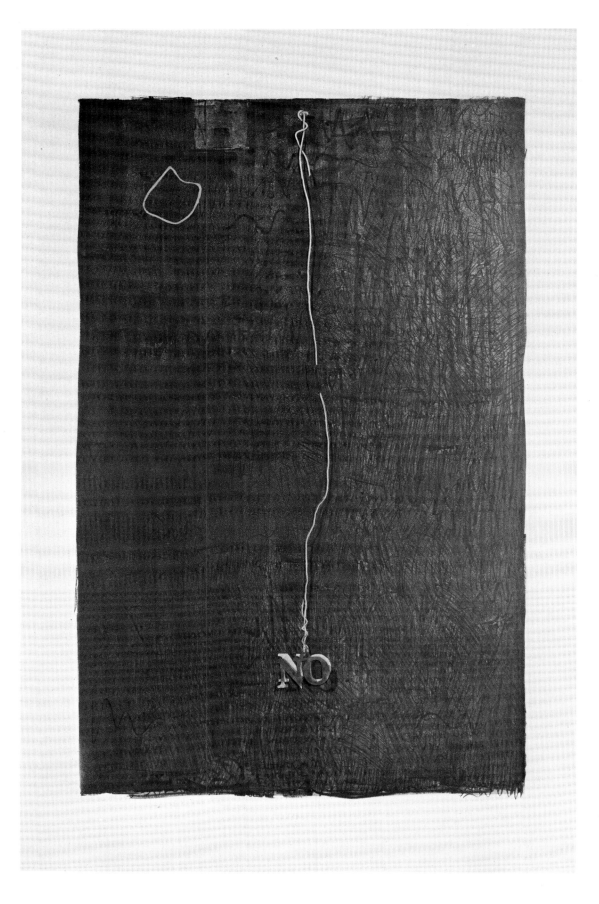

Jasper Johns, *No*, 1969

Jasper Johns, *Light Bulb*, 1969

40

Ken Price, *Figurine Cup VI*, 1970

Roy Lichtenstein, *Cathedral #5*, 1969

Roy Lichtenstein, *Peace Through Chemistry Bronze*, 1970

44

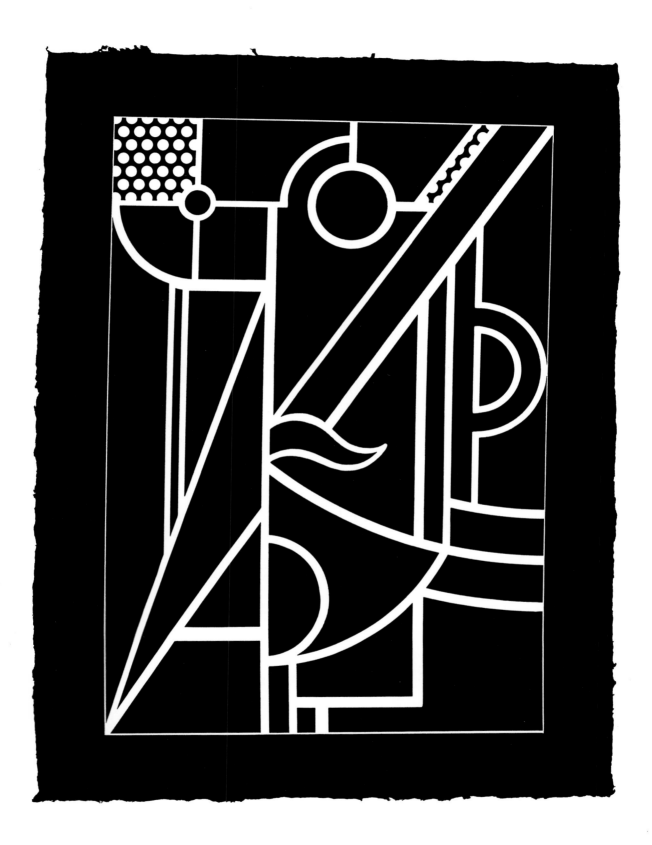

Roy Lichtenstein, *Modern Head #3*, 1970

Roy Lichtenstein, *Modern Head Relief,* 1970

46

Robert Rauschenberg, *Test Stone* #5A, 1967

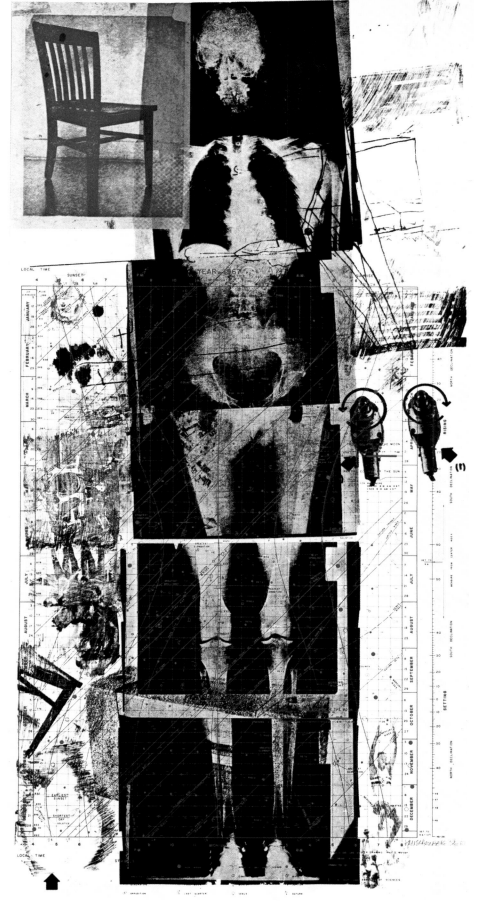

Robert Rauschenberg, *Booster*, 1967

48

Robert Rauschenberg, *Horn*, 1969

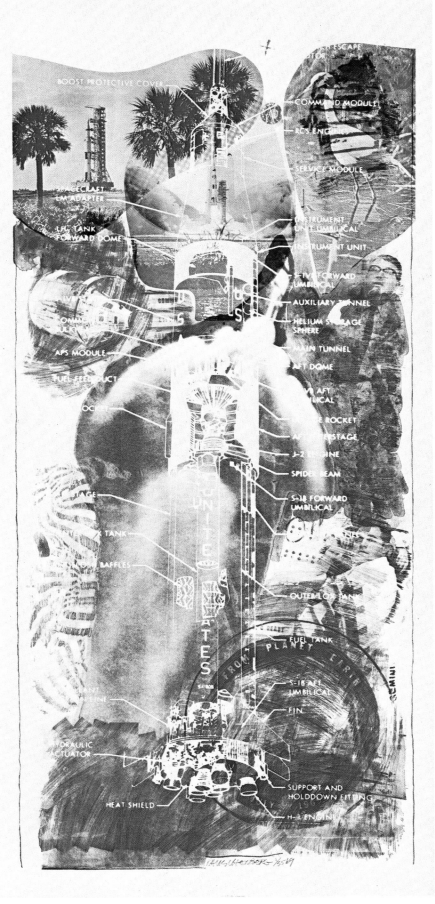

Robert Rauschenberg, *Sky Garden*, 1969

50

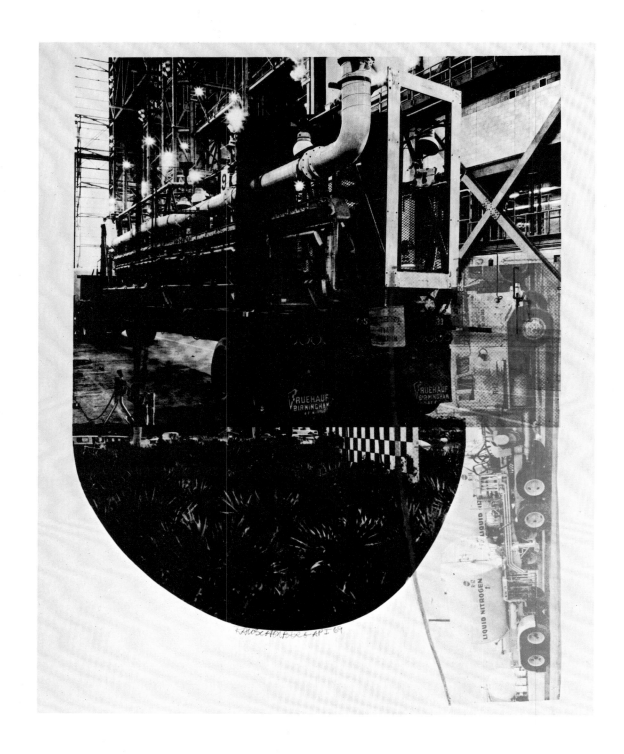

Robert Rauschenberg, *Tracks,* 1970

Robert Rauschenberg. *Cardbird Door*, 1971

Frank Stella, *Star of Persia I*, 1967

Frank Stella, *Quathlamba II*, 1968 (Top)   Frank Stella, *Empress of India I*, 1968 (Bottom)

54

Frank Stella, *Grid Stack,* 1970

Claes Oldenburg, *Profile Airflow*, 1969

58

Claes Oldenburg, *Double-Nose/Purse/Punching Bag/Ashtray*, 1970

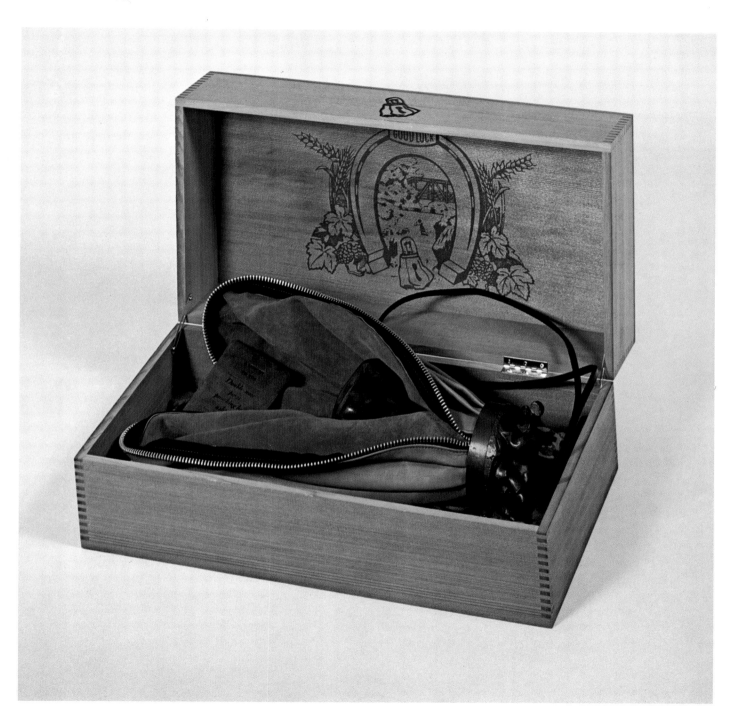

Claes Oldenburg, *Double-Nose/Purse/Punching Bag/Ashtray,* 1970

60

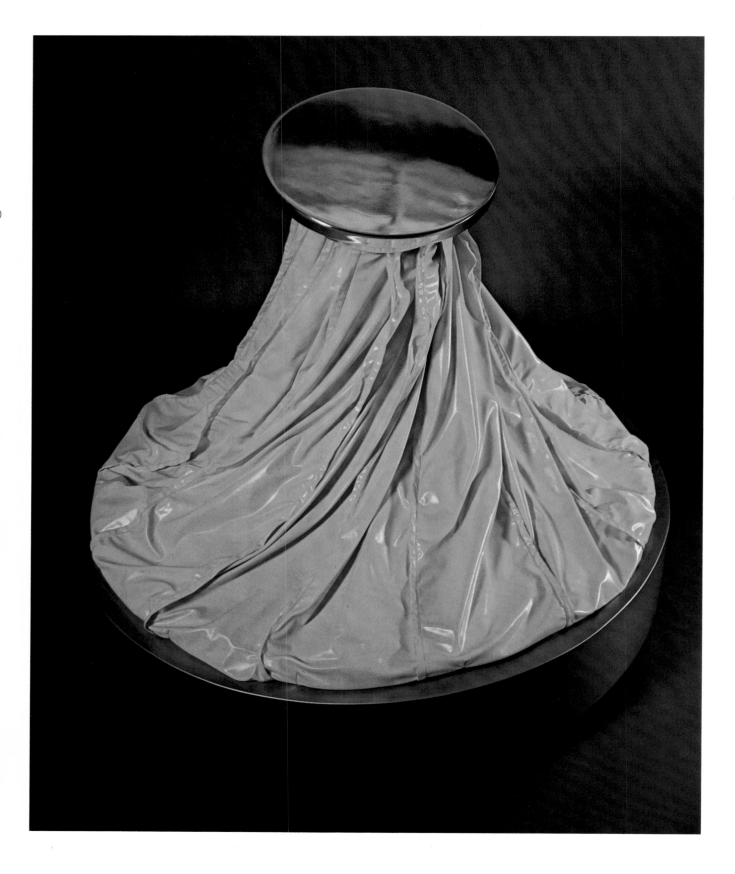

Claes Oldenburg, *Ice Bag-Scale B*, 1971

61

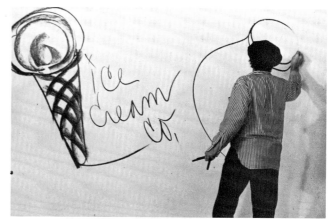

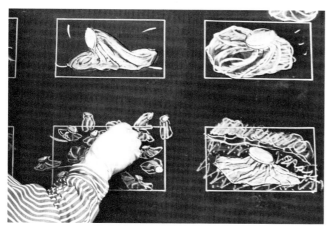

Sort of a Commercial for an Ice Bag, 1970

Ron Davis, *Cube III*, 1971

Don Judd, *Untitled*, 1971

Ellsworth Kelly, *Mirrored Concorde*, 1971

Ellsworth Kelly, *Blue/Yellow/Red*, 1970

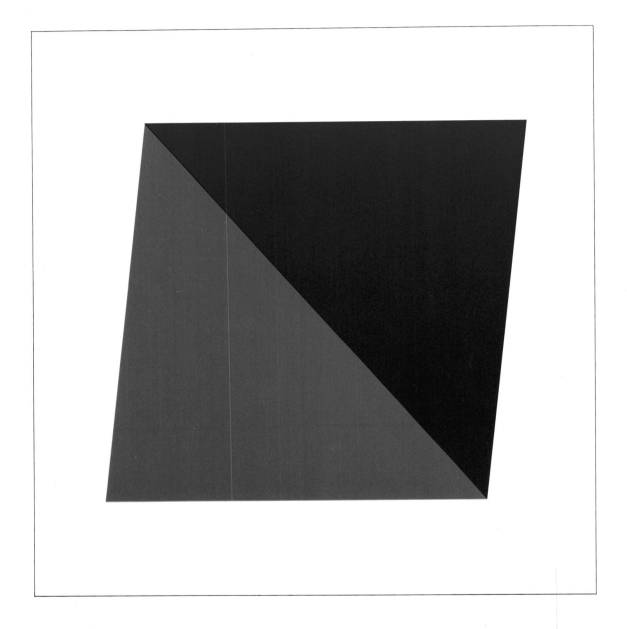

Ellsworth Kelly, *Blue/Green*, 1970

69

John Chamberlain, *Le Molé*, 1971

CATALOGUE RAISONNE

A chronological listing follows of the graphics and three-dimensional objects created at Gemini G.E.L. from 1966, when it began publishing, until February 1, 1971. The date indicated is that of publication. Dimensions are given in inches, height preceding width; for graphics, sheet size is given.

Each print bears either an embossed, dry stamped, or printed form of the chop mark of Gemini and a copyright symbol. All prints have a work number which is located next to the chop mark on the verso. The artist signs and numbers every print and may include a date and title. These appear with the chop mark in the lower right-hand corner of each print. Although cancellation copies are made for prints, none exists for any three-dimensional object; in all cases, the jigs, fixtures, molds, or tooling have been destroyed.

Listed below is an explanation of the terminology used by Gemini in its documentation records; abbreviations are the same as those found in the catalogue raisonné.

Edition

The number of prints published that are identical in appearance to the Right to Print proof; an edition of 50, for example, contains 50 identical prints numbered 1/50, 2/50, 3/50 etc.

AP Artist's Proofs

Proofs of good quality that closely match or equal the standards of the edition prints. These proofs are for the collections of the artist and publisher.

TP Trial Proofs

Black proofs pulled prior to the Right to Print proof, retained for their unique quality. These proofs usually do not resemble the edition prints.

RTP Right to Print

The first impression obtained during proofing that meets both the esthetic and technical standards of the artist and printer. It becomes the edition standard and is the property of the Master Printer.

PPII Printer's Proof II

A proof pulled for the printer who collaborated with the artist and the Master Printer in the creation and printing of the edition.

GEL Gemini Impressions

Impressions from each edition used solely for exhibition purposes. These prints are not for sale.

CTP Color Trial Proofs

First color proofs where sequence of color printing or colors are not completely resolved by the artist and printers. These proofs are different from the printed edition and exist only in the case of complex color prints.

PP Progressive Proofs

Proofs which show the breakdown of color separations in a given print.

State Prints

Prints in which the image of a printed or approved edition has been altered and printed as a separate edition. Each State Edition has its own proofs and work number. It is signed State I 1/10, 2/10, or State II 1/20, 2/20, etc.

SP Special Proof

A dedication print pulled outside of the edition.

WP Work Proofs

Impressions on which the artist paints or draws during the collaboration with the printer; often on different paper from the edition.

NCI National Council Impression

A special impression pulled from each of the eighteen editions which were partially funded by a research and development grant from the National Foundation on the Arts and Humanities.

C Cancellation Proof

The proof pulled after the printing element is cancelled by either the artist or the printer. Cancellation occurs to assure that no further proofs can be pulled after the edition has been printed. The printing image is fully inked and then defaced by the use of a sharp instrument or stone hone. The impression pulled of this defaced printing element documents the act and is signed and dated by the artist. If more than one State is printed, the cancellation proof is pulled after all States are printed.

AC Artist's Copies

The copies of a three-dimensional object retained by the artist.

PC Publisher's Copies

The copies of a three-dimensional object retained by the publisher.

1 1966   AD66-1146

Allan D'Arcangelo
Untitled

4 color lithograph
26″x26″ Rives BFK paper
Printed by Kenneth Tyler

Edition: 60 plus 11 AP,
4 TP, RTP, PPII, 2 GEL, C

WHITE LINE SQUARES (2 TO 17)

2 1966   JA66-1151

Josef Albers
White Line Square I

3 color lithograph
21″x21″ Arches paper
Printed by Bernard Bleha

Edition: 125 plus 15 AP,
10 TP, RTP, PPII, 2 GEL, C

3 1966   JA66-1152

Josef Albers
White Line Square II

3 color lithograph
21″x21″ Arches paper
Printed by Bernard Bleha

Edition: 125 plus 15 AP,
10 TP, RTP, PPII, 2 GEL, C

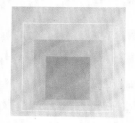

4 1966   JA66-1156

Josef Albers
White Line Square III

3 color lithograph
21″x21″ Arches paper
Printed by Bernard Bleha

Edition: 125 plus 10 AP,
5 TP, RTP, PPII, 2 GEL, 10 PP, C

5 1966   JA66-1157
Josef Albers
White Line Square IV

3 color lithograph
21″x21″ Arches paper
Printed by Bernard Bleha

Edition: 125 plus 15 AP,
5 TP, RTP, PPII, 2 GEL, 5 CTP, C

6 1966   JA66-1153
Josef Albers
White Line Square V

3 color lithograph
21″x21″ Arches paper
Printed by James Webb

Edition: 125 plus 15 AP,
5 TP, RTP, PPII, 2 GEL, C

7 1966   JA66-1155
Josef Albers
White Line Square VI

3 color lithograph
21″x21″ Arches paper
Printed by James Webb

Edition: 125 plus 10 AP,
5 TP, RTP, PPII, 2 GEL, C

8 1966   JA66-1158

Josef Albers
White Line Square VII

3 color lithograph
21″x21″ Arches paper
Printed by James Webb

Edition: 125 plus 15 AP, 5 TP, RTP,
PPII, 2 GEL, 6 CTP, 4 PP, C

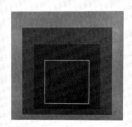

9 1966   JA66-1154
Josef Albers
White Line Square VIII

3 color lithograph
21″x21″ Arches paper
Printed by Bernard Bleha

Edition: 125 plus 10 AP,
TP, RTP, PPII, 2 GEL, 2 CTP, C

10 1966 JA66-1159

Josef Albers
White Line Square IX

3 color lithograph
21"x21" Arches paper
Printed by James Webb

Edition: 125 plus 10 AP,
RTP, PPII, 2 GEL, 10 PP, C

72

11 1966 JA66-1160

Josef Albers
White Line Square X

3 color lithograph
21"x21" Arches paper
Printed by Octavio Pereira

Edition: 125 plus 15 AP, RTP,
PPII, 2 GEL, 10 CTP, 6 PP, C

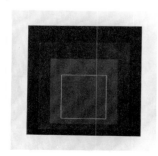

12 1966 JA66-1161

Josef Albers
White Line Square XI

3 color lithograph
21"x21" Arches paper
Printed by James Webb

Edition: 125 plus 10 AP,
5 TP, RTP, PPII, 2 GEL,
8 PP, 3 CTP, C

13 1966 JA66-1162

Josef Albers
White Line Square XII

3 color lithograph
21"x21" Arches paper
Printed by James Webb

Edition: 125 plus 10 AP, 5 TP,
RTP, PPII, 2 GEL, 5 PP, C

14 1966 JA66-1163

Josef Albers
White Line Square XIII

3 color lithograph
21"x21" Arches paper
Printed by James Webb

Edition: 125 plus 10 AP,
5 TP, RTP, PPII, 2 GEL, C

15 1966 JA66-1164

Josef Albers
White Line Square XIV

3 color lithograph
21"x21" Arches paper
Printed by James Webb

Edition: 125 plus 15 AP, 10 TP,
RTP, PPII, 2 GEL, 4 CTP, C

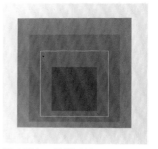

16 1966 JA66-1165

Josef Albers
White Line Square XV

3 color lithograph
21"x21" Arches paper
Printed by James Webb

Edition: 125 plus 15 AP,
10 TP, RTP, PPII, 2 GEL, C

17 1966 JA66-1166

Josef Albers
White Line Square XVI

3 color lithograph
21"x21" Arches paper
Printed by James Webb

Edition: 125 plus 10 AP, 5 TP,
RTP, PPII, 2 GEL, 2 PP, C

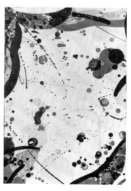

18 1966 SF66-1190

Sam Francis
Untitled

3 color lithograph
23½"x 15¾" Rives BFK paper
Printed by James Webb

Edition: 100 plus 5 AP, 5 TP,
RTP, PPII, 2 GEL, 5 CTP, C

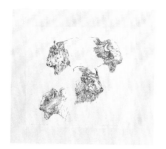

19 1966   WC66-1148

William Crutchfield
Buffalo Heads

1 color lithograph/watercolor
14½"x 15" China on Arches paper
Printed by George Page

Edition: 25 plus 5 AP,
TP, RTP, PPII, 2 GEL, C

20 1966   MR66-1194

Man Ray
Untitled

1 color lithograph
25½"x 22" Rives BFK paper
Printed by James Webb

Edition: 125 plus 15 AP,
5 TP, RTP, PPII, 2 GEL, C

21 1966   MR66-1195

Man Ray
Hands

2 color silkscreen
27"x 21" plexiglas (in frame)
Printed by Kenneth Tyler

Edition: 40 plus 10 AP,
6 TP, RTP, PPII, 2 GEL, C

22 1966   MR66-1196

Man Ray
One Hand

2 color silkscreen
27"x21" plexiglas (in frame)
Printed by Kenneth Tyler

Edition: 40 plus 10 AP,
6 TP, RTP, PPII, 2 GEL, C

23 1966   BS66-1197

Ben Shahn
Lavina

1 color lithograph
30"x22" Rives BFK paper
Printed by James Webb

Edition: 125 plus 10 AP,
5 TP, RTP, PPII, 2 GEL, C

24 1967   JR66-2001

Joe Raffaele
Boy Touching Man Touching Upper Lip

1 color lithograph
23"x28¼" German Etching paper
Printed by James Webb

Edition: 100 plus 10 AP,
4 TP, RTP, PPII, 2 GEL, C

25 1967   JA67-139

Josef Albers
White Line Square XVII

3 color lithograph
21"x21" Arches paper
Printed by James Webb

Edition: 125 plus 15 AP,
10 TP, RTP, PPII, 2 GEL, C

**BOOSTER AND 7 STUDIES
(26 TO 34)**

26 1967   RR67-101

Robert Rauschenberg
Test Stone #1

1 color lithograph
18"x14" Rives BFK paper
Printed by Octavio Pereira

Edition: 77 plus 7 AP,
4 TP, RTP, PPII, 2 GEL, C

27 1967   RR67-102

Robert Rauschenberg
Test Stone #2

1 color lithograph
41"x30" Rives BFK paper
Printed by Kenneth Tyler

Edition: 76 plus 10 AP,
4 TP, RTP, PPII, 2 GEL, C

28 1967 RR67-103

Robert Rauschenberg
Test Stone #3

2 color lithograph
23"x31" Barcham Green paper
Printed by James Webb

Edition: 71 plus 12 AP,
5 TP, RTP, PPII, 2 GEL, C

29 1967 RR67-104

Robert Rauschenberg
Test Stone #4

1 color lithograph
24"x34" Rives BFK paper
Printed by James Webb

Edition: 46 plus 5 AP,
5 TP, RTP, PPII, 2 GEL, C

30 1967 RR67-105

Robert Rauschenberg
Test Stone #5

2 color lithograph
25"x33" Rives BFK paper
Printed by Robert Bigelow

Edition: 30 plus 8 AP,
2 TP, RTP, PPII, 2 GEL, C

31 1967 RR67-140

Robert Rauschenberg
Test Stone #5A

3 color lithograph
25"x33" Rives BFK paper
Printed by Octavio Pereira

Edition: 27 plus 8 AP,
3 TP, RTP, PPII, 2 GEL, C

32 1967 RR67-106

Robert Rauschenberg
Booster

4 color lithograph/silkscreen
72"x35½" Curtis Rag paper
Printed by Kenneth Tyler

Edition: 38 plus 12 AP,
9 TP, RTP, PPII, 2 GEL, C

33 1967 RR67-107

Robert Rauschenberg
Test Stone #6

3 color lithograph
47"x35" Domestic Etching paper
Printed by Robert Bigelow

Edition: 44 plus 6 AP,
2 TP, RTP, PPII, 2 GEL, C

34 1967 RR67-108

Robert Rauschenberg
Test Stone #7

1 color lithograph
33"x48" Domestic Etching paper
Printed by Robert Bigelow

Edition: 38 plus 6 AP,
TP, RTP, PPII, 2 GEL, C

ENGLISH STILL LIFE SERIES (35 TO 40)

35 1967 JG67-118

Joe Goode
Glass at Top — Spoon on Bottom

2 color lithograph/silkscreen
22"x22" Rives BFK paper
Printed by James Webb

Edition: 3 plus RTP, C

36 1967 JG67-119

Joe Goode
Glass Lower Right — Spoon Upper Left

2 color lithograph/silkscreen
22"x22" Rives BFK paper
Printed by James Webb

Edition: 13 plus RTP, C

74

37 1967   JG67-120

Joe Goode
Glass Middle Left—Spoon Middle
Right

2 color lithograph/silkscreen
22″x22″ Rives BFK paper
Printed by James Webb

Edition: 4 plus RTP, C

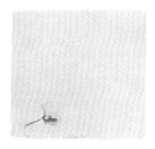

38 1967   JG67-121

Joe Goode
Glass and Spoon Lower Left

2 color lithograph/silkscreen
22″x22″ Rives BFK paper
Printed by James Webb

Edition: 5 plus RTP, C

39 1967   JG67-122

Joe Goode
Glass and Spoon Left Middle

2 color lithograph/silkscreen
22″x22″ Rives BFK paper
Printed by James Webb

Edition: 3 plus RTP, C

40 1967   JG67-123

Joe Goode
Spoon Upper Middle—Glass
Middle Right

2 color lithograph/silkscreen
22″x22″ Rives BFK paper
Printed by James Webb

Edition: 8 plus RTP, C

41 1967   JA67-161

John Altoon
Untitled

2 color lithograph
18″x20″ Rives BFK paper
Printed by James Webb

Edition: 100 plus 8 AP,
7 TP, RTP, PPII, 2 GEL, SP, C

VISTA SERIES
(42 TO 45)

42 1967   WC67-1177

William Crutchfield
At the Falls

2 color lithograph/watercolor
18″x31″ Arches paper
Printed by Octavio Pereira

Edition: 10 plus 5 AP,
2 TP, RTP, PPII, 2 GEL, C

43 1967   WC67-1178

William Crutchfield
Clipper Ship

1 color lithograph/watercolor
17″x31½″ German Etching paper
Printed by James Webb

Edition: 20 plus 3 AP,
2 TP, RTP, PPII, 2 GEL, C

44 1967   WC67-1179

William Crutchfield
Train on Bridge

1 color lithograph/watercolor
17″x31″ Barcham Green paper
Printed by Kenneth Tyler

Edition: 30 plus 4 AP,
TP, RTP, PPII, 2 GEL, C

45 1967   WC67-1180

William Crutchfield
Burning Mining Town

1 color lithograph/watercolor
17″x30¼″ Rives BFK paper
Printed by Robert de la Rocha

Edition: 11 plus 6 AP,
RTP, 2 GEL, 8 CTP, C

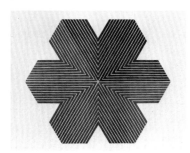

46 1967 FS67-110

Frank Stella
Star of Persia I

7 color lithograph
26"x31" English Vellum Graph paper
Printed by James Webb

Edition: 92 plus 9 AP, 7 TP, RTP,
PPII, 2 GEL, 6 CTP, 3 PP, C

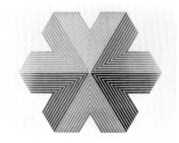

47 1967 FS67-111

Frank Stella
Star of Persia II

7 color lithograph
26"x31" English Vellum Graph paper
Printed by James Webb

Edition: 92 plus 10 AP, TP, RTP,
PPII, 2 GEL, 5 CTP, 2 PP, C

BLACK SERIES I (48 TO 56)

48 1967 FS67-129

Frank Stella
Clinton Plaza

2 color lithograph
15"x22" Barcham Green paper
Printed by Kenneth Tyler

Edition: 100 plus 9 AP,
RTP, PPII, 2 GEL, C

49 1967 FS67-130

Frank Stella
Arundel Castle

2 color lithograph
15"x22" Barcham Green paper
Printed by James Webb

Edition: 100 plus 9 AP,
RTP, PPII, 2 GEL, C

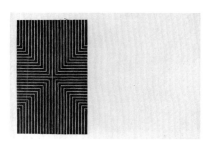

50 1967 FS67-131

Frank Stella
Die Fahne Hoch!

2 color lithograph
15"x22" Barcham Green paper
Printed by Kenneth Tyler

Edition: 100 plus 9 AP,
RTP, PPII, 2 GEL, C

51 1967 FS67-132

Frank Stella
Marriage of Reason and Squalor

2 color lithograph
15"x22" Barcham Green paper
Printed by Kenneth Tyler

Edition: 100 plus 9 AP,
RTP, PPII, 2 GEL, C

52 1967 FS67-133

Frank Stella
Tomlinson Court Park

2 color lithograph
15"x22" Barcham Green paper
Printed by Kenneth Tyler

Edition: 100 plus 9 AP,
RTP, PPII, 2 GEL, C

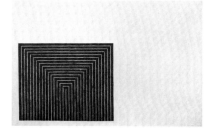

53 1967 FS67-134

Frank Stella
Getty Tomb

2 color lithograph
15"x22" Barcham Green paper
Printed by Kenneth Tyler

Edition: 100 plus 9 AP,
RTP, PPII, 2 GEL, C

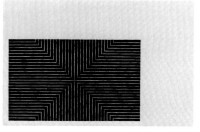

54 1967 FS67-135

Frank Stella
Arbeit Macht Frei

2 color lithograph
15"x22" Barcham Green paper
Printed by James Webb

Edition: 100 plus 9 AP,
RTP, PPII, 2 GEL, C

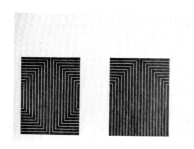

55 1967 FS67-136

Frank Stella
Club Onyx—Seven Steps

2 color lithograph
15"x22" Barcham Green paper
Printed by Kenneth Tyler

Edition: 100 plus 9 AP,
RTP, PPII, 2 GEL, C

56 1967 FS67-137

Frank Stella
Bethlehem's Hospital

2 color lithograph
15"x22" Barcham Green paper
Printed by Kenneth Tyler

Edition: 100 plus 9 AP,
RTP, PPII, 2 GEL, C

57 1967 ER67-149

Ed Ruscha
1984

2 color lithograph/watercolor
20"x25" Barcham Green paper
Printed by Charles Ritt

Edition: 60 plus 16 AP,
2 TP, RTP, PPII, 2 GEL, C

58 1967 WC67-1181

William Crutchfield
Old Jenny

2 color lithograph/watercolor
12"x19½" Rives BFK paper
Printed by Robert de la Rocha

Edition: 56 plus 9 AP,
2TP, RTP, PPII, 2 GEL, 2 CTP, C

59 1967 WC67-1182

William Crutchfield
Model T Ford

2 color lithograph/watercolor
12"x 19½" Rives BFK paper
Printed by James Webb

Edition: 56 plus 8 AP,
3 TP, RTP, PPII, 2 GEL, 2 CTP, C

60 1967 WC67-1183

William Crutchfield
Stage Coach

2 color lithograph/watercolor
12"x19½" Rives BFK paper
Printed by Charles Ritt

Edition: 56 plus 12 AP, 5 TP,
RTP, PPII, 2 GEL, 7 CTP, 2 PP, C

61 1967 WC67-1184

William Crutchfield
Fire Engine

2 color lithograph/watercolor
12"x19½" Rives BFK paper
Printed by Charles Ritt

Edition: 56 plus 8 AP, 3 TP, RTP,
PPII, 2 GEL, 2 PP, C

77

62 1967 WC67-1186

William Crutchfield
Riverboat

2 color lithograph/watercolor
12"x19½" Rives BFK paper
Printed by Robert de la Rocha

Edition: 56 plus 15 AP, 3 TP, RTP,
PPII, 2 GEL, 5 CTP, PP, C

63 1967 WC67-1187

William Crutchfield
Narrow Gauge Train

2 color lithograph/watercolor
12"x19½" Rives BFK paper
Printed by Robert de la Rocha

Edition: 56 plus 8 AP, 2 TP, RTP,
PPII, 2 GEL, 7 CTP, PP, C

64 1967   WC67-2002

William Crutchfield
Covered Wagons

2 color lithograph/watercolor
12″x19½″ Rives BFK paper
Printed by James Webb

Edition: 56 plus 12 AP, 5 TP, RTP,
PPII, 2 GEL, 2 CTP, PP, C

65 1967   WC67-2003

William Crutchfield
Clipper Ship

2 color lithograph/watercolor
12″x19½″ Rives BFK paper
Printed by Charles Ritt

Edition: 56 plus 8 AP, TP, RTP,
2 PPII, 2 GEL, CTP, PP, C

**BLACK SERIES II
(66 TO 73)**

66 1967   FS67-141

Frank Stella
Tuxedo Park

1 color lithograph
15″x22″ Barcham Green paper
Printed by James Webb

Edition: 100 plus 9 AP,
RTP, PPII, 2 GEL, C

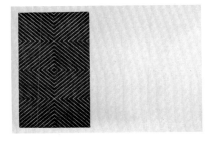

67 1967   FS67-142

Frank Stella
Gezira

1 color lithograph
15″x22″ Barcham Green paper
Printed by Robert de la Rocha

Edition: 100 plus 9 AP,
RTP, PPII, 2 GEL, C

68 1967   FS67-143

Frank Stella
Point of Pines

1 color lithograph
15″x22″ Barcham Green paper
Printed by Robert de la Rocha

Edition: 100 plus 9 AP,
RTP, PPII, 2 GEL, C

69 1967   FS67-144

Frank Stella
Zambesi

1 color lithograph
15″x22″ Barcham Green paper
Printed by Robert de la Rocha

Edition: 100 plus 9 AP,
5 TP, RTP, PPII, 2 GEL, C

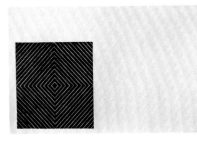

70 1967   FS67-145

Frank Stella
Jill

1 color lithograph
15″x22″ Barcham Green paper
Printed by Robert de la Rocha

Edition: 100 plus 9 AP,
RTP, PPII, 2 GEL, C

71 1967   FS67-146

Frank Stella
Delphine and Hippolyte

1 color lithograph
15″x22″ Barcham Green paper
Printed by James Webb

Edition: 100 plus 9 AP,
5 TP, RTP, PPII, 2 GEL, C

72 1967   FS67-147

Frank Stella
Gavotte

1 color lithograph
15″x22″ Barcham Green paper
Printed by James Webb

Edition: 100 plus 9 AP,
TP, RTP, PPII, 2 GEL, C

73 1967 FS67-148

Frank Stella
Turkish Mambo

1 color lithograph
15"x22" Barcham Green paper
Printed by James Webb

Edition: 100 plus 9 AP,
5 TP, RTP, PPII, 2 GEL, C

74 1967 FS67-159

Frank Stella
Irving Blum Memorial Edition

1 color lithograph
26"x31" English Vellum Graph paper
Printed by James Webb

Edition: 16 plus 3 AP,
2 TP, RTP, PPII, 2 GEL, C

V SERIES (75 TO 82)

75 1968 FS67-151

Frank Stella
Ifafa I

3 color lithograph
16¼"x22⅜" Lowell paper
Printed by James Webb

Edition: 100 plus 12 AP,
6 TP, RTP, PPII, 3 GEL, C

76 1968 FS67-152

Frank Stella
Itata

3 color lithograph
16¼"x22⅜" Lowell paper
Printed by James Webb

Edition: 100 plus 12 AP,
6 TP, RTP, PPII, 3 GEL, C

77 1968 FS67-153

Frank Stella
Ifafa II

3 color lithograph
16¼"x22⅜" Lowell paper
Printed by James Webb

Edition: 100 plus 12 AP,
6 TP, RTP, PPII, 3 GEL, C

78 1968 FS67-154

Frank Stella
Black Adder

4 color lithograph
16¼"x28⅞" Lowell paper
Printed by James Webb

Edition: 100 plus 14 AP,
6 TP, RTP, PPII, 3 GEL, C

79 1968 FS67-155

Frank Stella
Quathlamba I

4 color lithograph
16¼"x28⅞" Lowell paper
Printed by Charles Ritt

Edition: 100 plus 12 AP,
3 TP, RTP, PPII, 3 GEL, C

80 1968 FS67-156

Frank Stella
Quathlamba II

4 color lithograph
16¼"x28⅞" Lowell paper
Printed by James Webb

Edition: 100 plus 16 AP,
7 TP, RTP, PPII, 3 GEL, C

81 1968 FS67-157

Frank Stella
Empress of India I

5 color lithograph
16¼"x35⅜" Lowell paper
Printed by Charles Ritt

Edition: 100 plus 16 AP,
11 TP, RTP, PPII, 3 GEL, C

82 1968   FS67-158

Frank Stella
Empress of India II

5 color lithograph
16¼"x35⅜" Lowell paper
Printed by Charles Ritt

Edition: 100 plus 15 AP,
4 TP, RTP, PPII, 3 GEL, C

83 1967   WC67-1185

William Crutchfield
Tawny Owl   State I

2 color lithograph/watercolor
20"x14" Barcham Green paper
Printed by Octavio Pereira

Edition: 75 plus 7 AP,
TP, PPII, 3 GEL, CTP

Stone used for edition printing
WC67-1185A

84 1967   WC67-1185A

William Crutchfield
Tawny Owl   State II

3 color lithograph/watercolor
20"x14" Barcham Green paper
Printed by Octavio Pereira

Edition: 18 plus 4 AP, TP, RTP, C

85 1968   WT67-162

Wayne Thiebaud
Suckers   State I

1 color lithograph
16"x22" Rives BFK paper
Printed by Charles Ritt

Edition: 150 plus 11 AP,
10 TP, RTP, 3 GEL, 3 CTP, C

86 1968   WT67-162A

Wayne Thiebaud
Suckers   State II

1 color lithograph
16"x22" Rives BFK paper
Printed by Bruce Lowney

Edition: 150 plus 10 AP,
9 TP, PPII, 3 GEL, 2 CTP
Stone used for edition printing WT67-162

BLACK NUMERAL SERIES
(87 TO 96)

87 1968   JJ68-193

Jasper Johns
Figure 0

2 color lithograph
37"x30" Copperplate Deluxe paper
Printed by Charles Ritt

Edition: 70 plus 10 AP, 2 TP, RTP, PPII,
3 GEL. Plate and stone used
for color edition printing JJ68-202

88 1968   JJ68-192

Jasper Johns
Figure I

2 color lithograph
37"x30" Copperplate Deluxe paper
Printed by James Webb

Edition: 70 plus 10 AP, 2 TP, RTP, PPII,
3 GEL. Plate and Stone used
for color edition printing JJ68-200

89 1968   JJ68-198

Jasper Johns
Figure 2

2 color lithograph
37"x30" Copperplate Deluxe paper
Printed by Charles Ritt

Edition: 70 plus 10 AP, 3 TP, RTP, PPII,
3 GEL. Plate and Stone used
for color edition printing JJ68-206

90 1968   JJ68-194

Jasper Johns
Figure 3

2 color lithograph
37"x30" Copperplate Deluxe paper
Printed by Charles Ritt

Edition: 70 plus 10 AP, 3 TP, RTP, PPII,
3 GEL. Plate and Stone used
for color edition printing JJ68-207

91 1968   JJ68-190

Jasper Johns
Figure 4

2 color lithograph
37"x30" Copperplate Deluxe paper
Printed by James Webb

Edition: 70 plus 10 AP, 2 TP, RTP, PPII,
3 GEL. Plate and Stone used
for color edition printing JJ68-201

94 1968   JJ68-196

Jasper Johns
Figure 7

2 color lithograph
37"x30" Copperplate Deluxe paper
Printed by Kenneth Tyler

Edition: 70 plus 10 AP, 2 TP, RTP, PPII,
3 GEL. Plate and Stone used
for color edition printing JJ68-208

97 1968   JJ68-199

Jasper Johns
Gray Alphabets

4 color lithograph
60"x42" Special Arjomari paper
Printed by Charles Ritt

Edition: 59 plus 8 AP, RTP,
PPII, 3 GEL, 13 CTP, NCI, 2 C

81

REELS (B+C) (98 TO 103)

98 1968   RR68-171

Robert Rauschenberg
Storyline I

4 color lithograph
21½"x17" Rives BFK paper
Printed by Dan Gualdoni

Edition: 62 plus 10 AP,
4 TP, RTP, PPII, 3 GEL, C

92 1968   JJ68-195

Jasper Johns
Figure 5

2 color lithograph
37"x30" Copperplate Deluxe paper
Printed by James Webb

Edition: 70 plus 10 AP, 3 TP, RTP, PPII,
3 GEL. Plate and Stone used
for color edition printing JJ68-204

95 1968   JJ68-189

Jasper Johns
Figure 8

2 color lithograph
37"x30" Copperplate Deluxe paper
Printed by Charles Ritt

Edition: 70 plus 10 AP, 4 TP, RTP, PPII,
3 GEL. Plate and Stone used
for color edition printing JJ68-209

93 1968   JJ68-191

Jasper Johns
Figure 6

2 color lithograph
37"x30" Copperplate Deluxe paper
Printed by Charles Ritt

Edition: 70 plus 10 AP, 2 TP, RTP, PPII,
3 GEL. Plate and Stone used
for color edition printing JJ68-203

96 1968   JJ68-197

Jasper Johns
Figure 9

2 color lithograph
37"x30" Copperplate Deluxe paper
Printed by James Webb

Edition: 70 plus 10 AP, 2 TP, RTP,
PPII, 3 GEL. Plate and Stone used
for color edition printing JJ68-205

99 1968   RR68-173

Robert Rauschenberg
Storyline II

5 color lithograph
22"x18" Rives BFK paper
Printed by Charles Ritt

Edition: 59 plus 10 AP,
TP, RTP, PPII, 3 GEL, C

100 1968 RR68-172

Robert Rauschenberg
Storyline III

4 color lithograph
21½"x 17½" Rives BFK paper
Printed by James Webb

Edition: 72 plus 7 AP,
3 TP, RTP, PPII, 3 GEL, C

101 1968 RR68-174

Robert Rauschenberg
Love Zone

3 color lithograph
27"x23" Rives BFK paper
Printed by Charles Ritt

Edition: 60 plus 8 AP,
3 TP, RTP, PPII, 3 GEL, C

102 1968 RR68-175

Robert Rauschenberg
Flower Re-Run

3 color lithograph
23½"x18½" Rives BFK paper
Printed by Charles Ritt

Edition: 52 plus 9 AP,
5 TP, RTP, PPII, 3 GEL, C

103 1968 RR68-176

Robert Rauschenberg
Still

4 color lithograph
30"x22" Rives BFK paper
Printed by James Webb

Edition: 34 plus 7 AP,
4 TP, RTP, PPII, 3 GEL, C

NOTES (104 TO 115)

by Claes Oldenburg.

*27 pp., including 12 lithograph
plates, title page and colophon.
22¹¹/₁₆" x 15¾", unbound,
in black cloth box
with gray slipcase.*

104 1968 CO68-177

Claes Oldenburg

8 color lithograph
22¹¹/₁₆"x 15¾" Rives BFK paper
Printed by Dan Gualdoni

Edition: 100 plus 15 AP,
5 TP, RTP, PPII, 3 GEL, C

105 1968 CO68-178

Claes Oldenburg

6 color lithograph
22¹¹/₁₆"x 15¾" Rives BFK paper
Printed by James Webb

Edition: 100 plus 15 AP,
5 TP, RTP, PPII, 3 GEL, C

106 1968 CO68-179

Claes Oldenburg

6 color lithograph/embossing
22¹¹/₁₆"x 15¾" Rives BFK paper
Printed by Charles Ritt

Edition: 100 plus 15 AP,
5 TP, RTP, PPII, 3 GEL, C

107 1968 CO68-180

Claes Oldenburg

12 color lithograph/embossing
22¹¹/₁₆"x 15¾" Rives BFK paper
Printed by James Webb

Edition: 100 plus 15 AP,
5 TP, RTP, PPII, 3 GEL, C

108 1968   CO68-181

Claes Oldenburg

13 color lithograph/embossing
22¹¹/₁₆"x 15³/₄" Rives BFK paper
Printed by Robert de la Rocha

Edition: 100 plus 15 AP,
5 TP, RTP, PPII, 3 GEL, C

109 1968   CO68-182

Claes Oldenburg

11 color lithograph/embossing
22¹¹/₁₆"x 15³/₄" Rives BFK paper
Printed by Robert de la Rocha

Edition: 100 plus 15 AP,
5 TP, RTP, PPII, 3 GEL, C

110 1968   CO68-183

Claes Oldenburg

9 color lithograph
22¹¹/₁₆"x 15³/₄" Rives BFK paper
Printed by Robert de la Rocha

Edition: 100 plus 15 AP,
5 TP, RTP, PPII, 3 GEL, C

111 1968   CO68-184

Claes Oldenburg

9 color lithograph
22¹¹/₁₆"x 15³/₄" Rives BFK paper
Printed by James Webb

Edition: 100 plus 15 AP,
5 TP, RTP, PPII, 3 GEL, C

112 1968   CO68-185

Claes Oldenburg

6 color lithograph
22¹¹/₁₆"x 15³/₄" Rives BFK paper
Printed by James Webb

Edition: 100 plus 15 AP,
5 TP, RTP, PPII, 3 GEL, C

113 1968   CO68-186

Claes Oldenburg

6 color lithograph
22¹¹/₁₆"x 15³/₄" Rives BFK paper
Printed by James Webb

Edition: 100 plus 15 AP,
5 TP, RTP, PPII, 3 GEL, C

114 1968   CO68-187

Claes Oldenburg

9 color lithograph
22¹¹/₁₆"x 15³/₄" Rives BFK paper
Printed by Dan Gualdoni

Edition: 100 plus 15 AP,
5 TP, RTP, PPII, 3 GEL, C

115 1968   CO68-188

Claes Oldenburg

7 color lithograph
22¹¹/₁₆"x 15³/₄" Rives BFK paper
Printed by James Webb

Edition: 100 plus 15 AP,
5 TP, RTP, PPII, 3 GEL, C

**COLOR NUMERAL SERIES
(116 TO 125)**

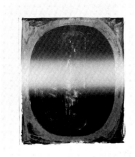

116 1969   JJ68-202

Jasper Johns
Figure 0

4 color lithograph
38"x31" Arjomari paper
Printed by Charles Ritt

Edition: 40 plus 11 AP, 10 TP, RTP, PPII,
3 GEL, 10 CTP, 4 PP, WP, 2 C

84

117 1969   JJ68-200

Jasper Johns
Figure 1

4 color lithograph
38"x31" Arjomari paper
Printed by Dan Freeman

Edition: 40 plus 9 AP, 6 TP, RTP,
PPII, 3 GEL, 4 CTP, 2 C

118 1969   JJ68-206

Jasper Johns
Figure 2

4 color lithograph
38"x31" Arjomari paper
Printed by James Webb

Edition: 40 plus 12 AP, 4 TP,
RTP, PPII, 3 GEL, 2 CTP, 2C

119 1969   JJ68-207

Jasper Johns
Figure 3

4 color lithograph
38"x31" Arjomari paper
Printed by Charles Ritt

Edition: 40 plus 8 AP, 4 TP,
RTP, PPII, 3 GEL, 2 CTP, 2C

120 1969   JJ68-201

Jasper Johns
Figure 4

4 color lithograph
38"x31" Arjomari paper
Printed by Charles Ritt

Edition: 40 plus 9 AP. 7 TP, RTP,
PPII, 3 GEL, 2 WP, 2C

121 1969   JJ68-204

Jasper Johns
Figure 5

4 color lithograph
38"x31" Arjomari paper
Printed by Charles Ritt

Edition: 40 plus 10 AP, 5 TP,
RTP, PPII, 3 GEL, 4 WP, 2C

122 1969   JJ68-203

Jasper Johns
Figure 6

4 color lithograph
38"x31" Arjomari paper
Printed by James Webb

Edition: 40 plus 12 AP, 4 TP,
RTP, PPII, 3 GEL, CTP, WP, 2 C

123 1969   JJ68-208

Jasper Johns
Figure 7

4 color lithograph
38"x31" Arjomari paper
Printed by Charles Ritt

Edition: 40 plus 9 AP, 8 TP,
RTP, PPII, 3 GEL, 4 PP, 2 C

124 1969   JJ68-209

Jasper Johns
Figure 8

4 color lithograph
38"x31" Arjomari paper
Printed by James Webb

Edition: 40 plus 9 AP, 4 TP,
RTP, PPII, 3 GEL, 2 WP, 2 C

125 1969   JJ68-205

Jasper Johns
Figure 9

4 color lithograph
38"x31" Arjomari paper
Printed by Charles Ritt

Edition: 40 plus 12 AP, 8 TP,
RTP, PPII, 3 GEL, 3 CTP, 2 C

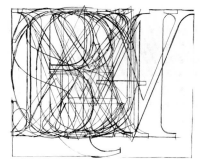

126 1969   JJ68-211

Jasper Johns
Alphabet

2 color lithograph
31"x37" German Etching paper
Printed by James Webb

Edition: 70 plus 9 AP,
TP, RTP, PPII, 3 GEL, WP, 2 C

127 1969   JJ69-216

Jasper Johns
Alphabet

Embossing
29¾"x37" Special Arches paper
Printed by Charles Ritt

Edition: 70 plus 9 AP,
RTP, PPII, 3 GEL , C

128 1969   JJ69-210

Jasper Johns
No

4 color lithograph with lead collage,
embossed, mounted to stretcher bar
and framed
56"x35" Arjomari paper
Printed by Charles Ritt

Edition: 80 plus 10 AP,
2 TP, RTP, PPII, 3 GEL, WP, 2 C

LEAD RELIEFS (129 TO 133)

129 1969   JJ69-217

Jasper Johns
High School Days

Lead Relief
23"x17" sheet lead and glass mirror
Printed by Kenneth Tyler

Edition: 60 plus 10 AP,
TP, RTP, 3 GEL, C

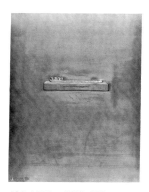

130 1969   JJ69-218

Jasper Johns
The Critic Smiles

Lead Relief
23"x17" sheet lead, gold casting
and tin leafing
Printed by Kenneth Tyler

Edition: 60 plus 10 AP,
2 TP, RTP, 3 GEL, C

131 1969   JJ69-219

Jasper Johns
Flag

Lead Relief
17"x23" sheet lead
Printed by Kenneth Tyler

Edition: 60 plus 10 AP,
RTP, 3 GEL, C

132 1969   JJ69-220

Jasper Johns
Light Bulb

Lead Relief
39"x17" sheet lead
Printed by Kenneth Tyler

Edition: 60 plus 10 AP, RTP, 3 GEL, C

85

133 1969   JJ69-222

Jasper Johns
Bread

Lead Relief
23"x17" cast lead, sheet lead,
paper and oil paint
Printed by Kenneth Tyler

Edition: 60 plus 10 AP, RTP, 3 GEL, C

EMBOSSED LINEAR CONSTRUCTIONS (134 TO 141)

134 1969   JA69-250

Josef Albers
Embossed Linear Construction 1-A

Embossing
20¹⁄₁₆"x26³⁄₃₂" Arches Watercolor paper
Printed by John Dill

Edition: 100 plus 10 AP,
RTP, PPII, 3 GEL, NCI, C

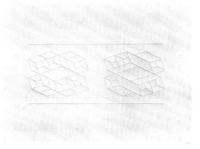

135 1969   JA69-253

Josef Albers
Embossed Linear Construction 1-B

Embossing
20¹/₁₆″x26³/₃₂″ Arches Watercolor paper
Printed by Dan Gualdoni

Edition: 100 plus 10 AP,
RTP, PPII, 3 GEL, NCI, C

136 1969   JA69-251

Josef Albers
Embossed Linear Construction 1-C

Embossing
20¹/₁₆″x26³/₃₂″ Arches Watercolor paper
Printed by Dan Gualdoni

Edition: 100 plus 10 AP,
RTP, PPII, 3 GEL, NCI, C

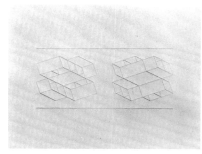

137 1969   JA69-252

Josef Albers
Embossed Linear Construction 1-D

Embossing
20¹/₁₆″x26³/₃₂″ Arches Watercolor paper
Printed by John Dill

Edition: 100 plus 10 AP,
RTP, PPII, 3 GEL, NCI, C

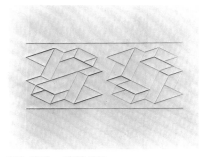

138 1969   JA69-255

Josef Albers
Embossed Linear Construction 2-A

Embossing
20¹/₁₆″x26³/₃₂″ Arches Watercolor paper
Printed by Tim Isham

Edition: 100 plus 10 AP,
RTP, PPII, 3 GEL, NCI, C

139 1969   JA69-256

Josef Albers
Embossed Linear Construction 2-B

Embossing
20¹/₁₆″x26³/₃₂″ Arches Watercolor paper
Printed by Dan Gualdoni

Edition: 100 plus 10 AP,
RTP, PPII, 3 GEL, NCI, C

140 1969   JA69-254

Josef Albers
Embossed Linear Construction 2-C

Embossing
20¹/₁₆″x26³/₃₂″ Arches Watercolor paper
Printed by Dan Gualdoni

Edition: 100 plus 10 AP,
RTP, PPII, 3 GEL, NCI, C

141 1969   JA69-257

Josef Albers
Embossed Linear Construction 2-D

Embossing
20¹/₁₆″x26³/₃₂″ Arches Watercolor paper
Printed by Dan Gualdoni

Edition: 100 plus 10 AP,
RTP, PPII, 3 GEL, NCI, C

**CATHEDRAL SERIES
(142 TO 149)**

142 1969   RL69-225

Roy Lichtenstein
Cathedral #1

2 color lithograph/silkscreen
48½″x32½″ Special Arjomari paper
Printed by Robert de la Rocha

Edition: 75 plus 10 AP,
RTP, PPII, 3 GEL, C

143 1969   RL69-226

Roy Lichtenstein
Cathedral #2

2 color lithograph
48½″x32½″ Special Arjomari paper
Printed by Stuart Henderson

Edition: 75 plus 10 AP,
RTP, PPII, 3 GEL, C

144 1969   RL69-227

Roy Lichtenstein
Cathedral #3

1 color lithograph
48½"x32½" Special Arjomari paper
Printed by Stuart Henderson

Edition: 75 plus 10 AP,
RTP, PPII, 3 GEL, C

145 1969   RL69-228

Roy Lichtenstein
Cathedral #4

2 color lithograph
48½"x32½" Special Arjomari paper
Printed by Charles Ritt

Edition: 75 plus 10 AP,
RTP, PPII, 3 GEL, C

146 1969   RL69-229

Roy Lichtenstein
Cathedral #5

2 color lithograph
48½"x32½" Special Arjomari paper
Printed by Dan Freeman

Edition: 75 plus 10 AP,
TP, RTP, PPII, 3 GEL, C

147 1969   RL69-230

Roy Lichtenstein
Cathedral #6

2 color lithograph
48½"x32½" Special Arjomari paper
Printed by Dan Freeman

Edition: 75 plus 10 AP,
5TP, RTP, PPII, 3 GEL, C

148 1969   RL69-230A

Roy Lichtenstein
Cathedral #6   State I

2 color lithograph
48½"x32½" Special Arjomari paper
Printed by Stuart Henderson

Edition: 13 plus RTP. Plates used
for edition printing RL69-230

149 1969   RL69-230B

Roy Lichtenstein
Cathedral #6   State II

2 color lithograph
48½"x32½" Special Arjomari paper
Printed by Bob Petersen

Edition: 13 plus RTP. Plates used
for edition printing RL69-230

**HAYSTACK SERIES
(150 TO 159)**

150 1969   RL69-231

Roy Lichtenstein
Haystack #1

2 color lithograph/silkscreen
20⅝"x30¾" Rives BFK paper
Printed by Stuart Henderson

Edition: 100 plus 10 AP,
RTP, PPII, 3 GEL, C

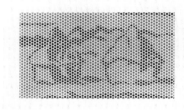

151 1969   RL69-232

Roy Lichtenstein
Haystack #2

3 color lithograph/silkscreen
20⅝"x30¾" Rives BFK paper
Printed by Stuart Henderson

Edition: 100 plus 10 AP,
RTP, PPII, 3 GEL, C

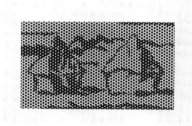

152 1969   RL69-233

Roy Lichtenstein
Haystack #3

3 color lithograph/silkscreen
20⅝"x30¾" Rives BFK paper
Printed by Stuart Henderson

Edition: 100 plus 10 AP,
RTP, PPII, 3 GEL, C

153 1969   RL69-234

Roy Lichtenstein
Haystack #4

3 color lithograph/silkscreen
20⅝"x30¾" Rives BFK paper
Printed by Stuart Henderson

Edition: 100 plus 10 AP,
RTP, PPII, 3 GEL, C

154 1969   RL69-235

Roy Lichtenstein
Haystack #5

3 color lithograph/silkscreen
20⅝"x30¾" Rives BFK paper
Printed by Richard Wilke

Edition: 100 plus 10 AP,
RTP, PPII, 3 GEL, C

155 1969   RL69-236

Roy Lichtenstein
Haystack #6

2 color lithograph
20⅝"x30¾" Rives BFK paper
Printed by Dan Gualdoni

Edition: 100 plus 10 AP,
RTP, PPII, 3 GEL, C

156 1969   RL69-236A

Roy Lichtenstein
Haystack #6 State I

2 color lithograph
20⅝"x30¾" Rives BFK paper
Printed by Dan Gualdoni

Edition: 13 plus RTP
Plates used for edition printing
RL69-236

157 1969   RL69-236B

Roy Lichtenstein
Haystack #6 State II

2 color lithograph
20⅝"x30¾" Rives BFK paper
Printed by Stuart Henderson

Edition: 13 plus RTP
Plates used for edition printing
RL69-236

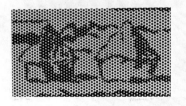

158 1969   RL69-236C

Roy Lichtenstein
Haystack #6 State III

2 color lithograph
20⅝"x30¾" Rives BFK paper
Printed by Stuart Henderson

Edition: 13 plus RTP
Plates used for edition printing
RL69-236

159 1969   RL69-237

Roy Lichtenstein
Haystack #7

1 color embossing
20⅝"x30¾" Special Arches paper
Printed by Charles Ritt

Edition: 100 plus 10 AP,
RTP, PPII, 3 GEL, C

STONED MOON SERIES (160 TO 176)

160 1969   RR69-272

Robert Rauschenberg
Trust Zone

3 color lithograph
40"x33" Special Rives paper
Printed by Dan Freeman

Edition: 65 plus 10 AP,
RTP, PPII, 3 GEL, SP, C

161 1969   RR69-273

Robert Rauschenberg
Shell

2 color lithograph
32⅛"x26" Special Arches paper
Printed by Tim Isham

Edition: 70 plus 6 AP,
3 TP, RTP, PPII, 3 GEL, SP, C

162 1969   RR69-276

Robert Rauschenberg
Horn

1 color lithograph
44¼″x34″ Special Rives paper
Printed by Charles Ritt

Edition: 58 plus 6 AP,
3 TP, RTP, PPII, 3 GEL, SP, C

163 1969   RR69-279

Robert Rauschenberg
Earth Tie

1 color lithograph
48″x34″ Arches Cover paper
Printed by Charles Ritt

Edition: 48 plus 6 AP,
2 TP, RTP, PPII, 3 GEL, SP, C

164 1969   RR69-280A

Robert Rauschenberg
Arena I   State I

1 color lithograph
47″x32″ Arches Cover paper
Printed by Dan Freeman

Edition: 12 plus 5 AP, RTP
Stone used for edition printing
RR69-280B

165 1969   RR69-280B

Robert Rauschenberg
Arena II   State II

1 color lithograph
47″x32″ Arches Cover paper
Printed by Dan Freeman

Edition: 50 plus 8 AP,
TP, RTP, PPII, 3 GEL, SP, C

166 1969   RR69-282

Robert Rauschenberg
Sack

5 color lithograph
40″x28″ Special Arjomari paper
Printed by Dan Freeman

Edition: 60 plus 10 AP,
RTP, PPII, 3 GEL, SP, C

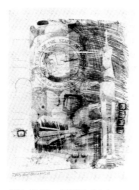

167 1969   RR69-284

Robert Rauschenberg
Marsh

1 color lithograph
35½″x25″ Arches Cover paper
Printed by Dan Freeman

Edition: 60 plus 6 AP,
RTP, PPII, 3 GEL, SP, C

168 1969   RR69-285

Robert Rauschenberg
Loop

1 color lithograph
33″x28″ Rives BFK paper
Printed by Charles Ritt

Edition: 79 plus 6 AP,
TP, RTP, PPII, 3 GEL, SP, C

169 1969   RR69-287

Robert Rauschenberg
Earth Crust

2 color lithograph
34″x25″ Arches Cover paper
Printed by Andrew Vlady

Edition: 42 plus 6 AP,
TP, RTP, PPII, 3 GEL, SP, C

170 1969   RR69-290

Robert Rauschenberg
Moon Rose

1 color lithograph
51″x35″ Arches Cover paper
Printed by Stuart Henderson

Edition: 47 plus 6 AP,
RTP, PPII, 3 GEL, SP, C

171 1969   RR69-292

Robert Rauschenberg
Medallion

1 color lithograph
32"x25½" Rives BFK paper
Printed by Charles Ritt

Edition: 48 plus 6 AP,
RTP, PPII, 3 GEL, SP, C

172 1969   RR69-297

Robert Rauschenberg
Rack

1 color lithograph
30"x24½" Rives BFK paper
Printed by Charles Ritt

Edition: 54 plus 6 AP,
RTP, PPII, 3 GEL, SP, C

173 1969   RR69-299

Robert Rauschenberg
Banner

4 color lithograph
54½"x36" Special Arjomari
Printed by Timothy Huchthausen

Edition: 40 plus 6 AP,
5 TP, RTP, PPII, 3 GEL, SP, C

174 1969   RR69-300

Robert Rauschenberg
Waves

1 color lithograph
89"x42" Special Arjomari paper
Printed by Kenneth Tyler

Edition: 27 plus 6 AP,
RTP, 3 GEL, SP, C

175 1969   RR69-301

Robert Rauschenberg
Sky Garden

6 color lithograph/silkscreen
89"x42" Special Arjomari paper
Printed by Kenneth Tyler, Charles Ritt

Edition: 35 plus 6 AP, 2 TP, RTP, PPII,
3 GEL, 15 CTP, 2 SP, 6 WP, NCI, C

176 1969   RR69-302

Robert Rauschenberg
Brake

1 color lithograph
42"x29" Arches Cover paper
Printed by Bob Peterson

Edition: 60 plus 8 AP,
RTP, PPII, 3 GEL, SP, C

177 1969   WC69-271

William Crutchfield
Reticulated Giraffe

1 color lithograph
18"x14" Rives BFK paper
Printed by Charles Ritt

Edition: 16 plus 6 AP, RTP, PPII
Stone not cancelled—dedicated and
sealed by artist; in collection of
Arjomari, France.

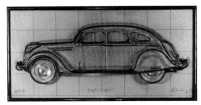

178 1969   CO68-304

Claes Oldenburg
Profile Airflow

Molded polyurethane relief over
2 color lithograph 33½"x65½"
Polyurethane and Special Arjomari
paper mounted on wood stretcher bars
and framed in aluminum
Collaborators: Kenneth Tyler, Jeff
Sanders, Richard Wilke

Edition: 75 plus 6 AP, 3 TP,
RTP, PPII, 3 GEL, C

179 1970   CO70-2004

Claes Oldenburg
Ice Bag—Scale A

Programmed kinetic sculpture
18' diameter rising to 16'

Red polyvinyl material,
lacquered wood, hydraulic
and mechanical movements
Collaborators: Kenneth Tyler and
Krofft Enterprises

Original sculpture created for
Art and Technology Exhibition,
United States Pavilion, 1970 World's
Fair, Osaka, Japan.

Signature, chop, copyright on metal
plate mounted inside

180 1970   CO70-309

Claes Oldenburg
Ice Bag

1 color lithograph
16"x22" Arches paper
Printed by Kenneth Tyler

Edition: 27 plus 4 AP,
RTP, 3 GEL, C

181 1970

Claes Oldenburg
Sort of a Commercial for an Ice Bag

16 mm color sound film

Producer: Gemini G.E.L.
Director: Michel Hugo

Cinematographer: Eric Saarinen
Editor: John Hoffman
Sound: Howard Chesley

Edition: unlimited

182 1970   CO70-310

Claes Oldenburg
Typewriter Eraser

3 color lithograph
12¼"x9½" Rives paper
Printed by Charles Ritt

Edition: 100 plus 20 AP,
RTP, PPII, 3 GEL, C

**STONED MOON SERIES
(183 TO 188)**

183 1970   RR69-275

Robert Rauschenberg
Sky Hook

1 color lithograph
48"x34" Special Arjomari paper
Printed by Charles Ritt

Edition: 52 plus 7 AP,
RTP, PPII, 3 GEL, SP, C

184 1970   RR69-283

Robert Rauschenberg
Sky Rite

1 color lithograph
33"x23" Arches Cover paper
Printed by Ron Adams

Edition: 56 plus 6 AP,
RTP, PPII, 3 GEL, SP, C

185 1970   RR69-288

Robert Rauschenberg
Post

2 color lithograph
34"x26" Arches Cover paper
Printed by Bob Peterson

Edition: 44 plus 6 AP,
RTP, PPII, 3 GEL, SP, C

186 1970   RR69-289

Robert Rauschenberg
Spore

2 color lithograph
34"x24" Arches Cover paper
Printed by Tim Isham

Edition: 50 plus 7 AP,
2 TP, RTP, PPII, 3 GEL, SP, C

187 1970 RR69-293

Robert Rauschenberg
Fuse

1 color lithograph
38"x26" Arches Cover paper
Printed by Ron Adams

Edition: 63 plus 8 AP,
RTP, PPII, 3 GEL, SP, C

188 1970 RR69-294

Robert Rauschenberg
Tilt

2 color lithograph
27½"x22¼" Rives BFK paper
Printed by Timothy Huchthausen

Edition: 60 plus 6 AP,
RTP, PPII, 3 GEL, SP, C

189 1970 JJ69-221

Jasper Johns
Numerals

Lead Relief
30"x23½" sheet lead
Printed by Kenneth Tyler, Jeff Sanders,
George Page

Edition: 60 plus 9 AP,
RTP, 3 GEL, NC I, C

190 1970 RL70-240

Roy Lichtenstein
Peace Through Chemistry I

5 color lithograph/silkscreen
37¾"x63½" Special Arjomari paper
Printed by Charles Ritt

Edition: 32 plus 6 AP,
RTP, PPII, 3 GEL, C

191 1970 RL70-241

Roy Lichtenstein
Peace Through Chemistry III

1 color lithograph
37¾"x63½" Special Arjomari paper
Printed by Ron Olds

Edition: 16 plus 6 AP,
RTP, PPII, 3 GEL, C

192 1970 RL70-242

Roy Lichtenstein
Peace Through Chemistry IV

3 color lithograph
30"x50" Special Arjomari paper
Printed by Tim Isham

Edition: 56 plus 6 AP,
RTP, PPII, 3 GEL, C

**FIGURINE CUP SERIES
(193 TO 198)**

193 1970 KP69-265

Ken Price
Figurine Cup I

6 color lithograph
22"x18" Special Arjomari paper
Printed by Charles Ritt

Edition: 59 plus 6 AP,
RTP, PPII, 3 GEL, C

194 1970 KP69-268

Ken Price
Figurine Cup II

8 color lithograph
22"x18" Special Arjomari paper
Printed by Timothy Huchthausen

Edition: 60 plus 6 AP,
TP, RTP, PPII, 3 GEL, C

195 1970 KP69-267

Ken Price
Figurine Cup III

7 color offset litho/silkscreen
18½"x15" Special Arjomari paper
Printed by Bob Blair

Edition: 63 plus 6 AP,
RTP, PPII, 3 GEL, C

196 1970   KP70-264

Ken Price
Figurine Cup IV

5 color lithograph/silkscreen
22"x18" Special Arjomari paper
Printed by Andrew Vlady

Edition: 61 plus 6 AP,
TP, RTP, PPII, 3 GEL, C

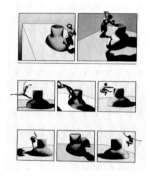

197 1970   KP70-269

Ken Price
Figurine Cup V

10 color lithograph
22"x18" Special Arjomari paper
Printed by Dan Freeman

Edition: 60 plus 9 AP,
RTP, PPII, 3 GEL, C

198 1970   KP69-266

Ken Price
Figurine Cup VI

10 color lithograph/silkscreen
22"x18" Special Arjomari paper
Printed by Charles Ritt

Edition: 63 plus 8 AP,
2 TP, RTP, PPII, 3 GEL, C

199 1970   RR69-271

Robert Rauschenberg
Bait

4 color lithograph
35¼"x26¼" Special Arjomari paper
Printed by Timothy Huchthausen

Edition: 45 plus 6 AP,
TP, RTP, PPII, 3 GEL, SP, C

200 1970   RR69-274

Robert Rauschenberg
Tracks

4 color lithograph
44"x35" Special Arjomari paper
Printed by Stuart Henderson

Edition: 54 plus 6 AP,
RTP, PPII, 3 GEL, SP, C

201 1970   RR70-277

Robert Rauschenberg
White Walk

3 color lithograph
42¼"x29½" Special Arjomari paper
Printed by Dan Freeman

Edition: 53 plus 6 AP,
RTP, PPII, 3 GEL, SP, C

202 1970   RR69-278

Robert Rauschenberg
Ape

3 color lithograph
46"x33" Special Arjomari paper
Printed by Ron Olds

Edition: 46 plus 6 AP,
RTP, PPII, 3 GEL, SP, WP, C

93

203 1970   RR69-286

Robert Rauschenberg
Air Pocket

1 color lithograph
36"x51" Special Arjomari paper
Printed by Bob Petersen

Edition: 47 plus 6 AP,
RTP, PPII, 3 GEL, SP, C

204 1970   RR69-291

Robert Rauschenberg
Ghost

2 color lithograph
34"x25½" Rives BFK paper
Printed by Kenneth Tyler

Edition: 2 plus 2 AP, RTP,
no cancellation, stone cracked

205 1970   RR69-298

Robert Rauschenberg
Hybrid

5 color lithograph
54½"x36" Special Arjomari paper
Printed by Charles Ritt

Edition: 52 plus 6 AP,
TP, RTP, PPII, 3 GEL, SP, C

206 1970   RR69-303

Robert Rauschenberg
Local Means

4 color lithograph
32³/₈"x43⁵/₁₆" Special Arjomari paper
Printed by Charles Ritt

Edition: 11 plus RTP,
PPII, 2 WP, C

207 1970   RR70-306

Robert Rauschenberg
Strawboss

2 color lithograph
30"x22" Special Arjomari paper
Printed by Tim Isham

Edition: 50 plus 6 AP,
RTP, PPII, 3 GEL, SP, C

208 1970   RR69-307

Robert Rauschenberg
Score

3 color lithograph
26"x19½" Rives BFK paper
Printed by Timothy Huchthausen

Edition: 75 plus 16 AP,
RTP, PPII, 3 GEL, SP, C

209 1970   RL70-2000

Roy Lichtenstein
Untitled Head I

3-dimensional object
25⁵/₈"x10¼"x³/₈" solid brass

Collaborators: Kenneth Tyler,
Jeff Sanders, Herbert Tomkins

Edition: 75
Signature, edition no., chop,
copyright on copper plate
inside base

210 1970   RL70-2001

Roy Lichtenstein
Untitled Head II

3-dimensional object
30" (high) California English Walnut
Collaborators: Kenneth Tyler,
Jeff Sanders, Herbert Tomkins

Edition: 30 plus TP
Signature, edition no., chop,
copyright on copper plate inside base

211 1970   AA68-215

Anni Albers
TR I

3 color lithograph
22"x23½" Rives paper
Printed by Stuart Henderson

Edition: 44 plus 6 AP,
TP, RTP, PPII, 3 GEL, 2 CTP, C

212 1970   AA70-216

Anni Albers
TRII

3 color lithograph
22"x 23½" Special Arjomari paper
Printed by Stuart Henderson

Edition: 45 plus 6 AP,
RTP, PPII, 3 GEL, C

94

213 1970   FS70-311

Frank Stella
Newstead Abbey

3 color lithograph/silkscreen
16"x22" Special Arjomari paper
Printed by Andrew Vlady

Edition: 75 plus 6 AP,
RTP, PPII, 3 GEL, C

214 1970   FS70-312

Frank Stella
Marquis de Portago

3 color lithograph/silkscreen
16"x22" Special Arjomari paper
Printed by Stuart Henderson

Edition: 75 plus 6 AP,
RTP, PPII, 3 GEL, C

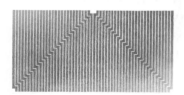

215 1970   FS70-313

Frank Stella
Union Pacific

3 color lithograph/silkscreen
16"x22" Special Arjomari paper
Printed by Charles Ritt

Edition: 75 plus 6 AP,
RTP, PPII, 3 GEL, C

216 1970   FS70-314

Frank Stella
Six Mile Bottom

3 color lithograph/silkscreen
16"x22" Special Arjomari paper
Printed by Andrew Vlady

Edition: 75 plus 6 AP,
RTP, PPII, 3 GEL, C

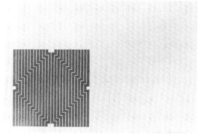

217 1970   FS70-315

Frank Stella
Averroes

3 color lithograph/silkscreen
16"x22" Special Arjomari paper
Printed by Timothy Huchthausen

Edition: 75 plus 6 AP,
RTP, PPII, 3 GEL, C

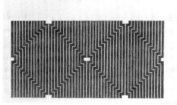

218 1970   FS70-316

Frank Stella
Casa Cornu

3 color lithograph/silkscreen
16"x22" Special Arjomari paper
Printed by Ron McPherson

Edition: 75 plus 6 AP,
RTP, PPII, 3 GEL, C

219 1970   FS70-317

Frank Stella
Luis Miguel Dominguin

3 color lithograph/silkscreen
16"x22" Special Arjomari paper
Printed by Ron Adams

Edition: 75 plus 6 AP,
RTP, PPII, 3 GEL, C

95

220 1970   FS70-318

Frank Stella
Avicenna

3 color lithograph/silkscreen
16"x22" Special Arjomari paper
Printed by Ron McPherson

Edition: 75 plus 6 AP,
RTP, PPII, 3 GEL, C

221 1970   FS70-319

Frank Stella
Kingsbury Run

3 color lithograph/silkscreen
16"x22" Special Arjomari paper
Printed by Ron McPherson

Edition: 75 plus 6 AP,
RTP, PPII, 3 GEL, C

222 1970   RL70-2002

Roy Lichtenstein
Peace Through Chemistry Bronze

3-dimensional object
27¼"x46¼"x1¼" bronze
Collaborators: Kenneth Tyler,
Jeff Sanders, Tom Papaleo

Edition: 38 plus 2 TP
Signature, edition no., chop,
copyright stamped on lower right edge

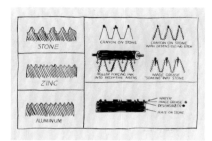

223 1970   RL70-329

Roy Lichtenstein
Litho/Litho

4 color lithograph
35"x48" Special Arjomari paper
Printed by James Webb

Edition: 54 plus 7 AP,
RTP, PPII, 3 GEL, C

224 1970   CO68-304A

Claes Oldenburg
Red State Profile Airflow

3-dimensional object
32"x64"x2" (plexiglas base:
34"x79"x24") molded polyurethane
relief over silkscreened plexiglas in
aluminum frame
Collaborators: Kenneth Tyler, Jeff
Sanders, George Page
Signature, chop, copyright on plate
mounted on base

STACKS (225 TO 227)

225 1970   FS70-351

Frank Stella
Grid Stack

1 color lithograph
45⅞"x35⅛" Special Arjomari paper
Printed by Ron Olds

Edition: 50 plus 7 AP,
2 TP, RTP, PPII, 3 GEL, C

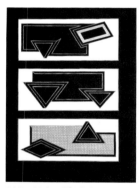

226 1970   FS70-352

Frank Stella
Black Stack

1 color lithograph
40¾"x29¼" Special Arjomari paper
Printed by Ron Adams

Edition: 56 plus 7 AP,
3 TP, RTP, PPII, 3 GEL, C

227 1970   FS70-353

Frank Stella
Pastel Stack

41 color silkscreen
41"x28" English Vellum Graph paper
Printed by Adolf Rischner

Edition: 100 plus 15 AP,
RTP, PPII, 3 GEL, 10 CTP, C

228 1970   FS70-362A

Frank Stella
Referendum '70

7 color silkscreen
40"x40" Special Arjomari paper
Printed by Jeff Wasserman

Edition: 150. There exists a signed and
numbered edition of same image
without Referendum '70 type.

229 1970   FS70-362

Frank Stella
Referendum '70

6 color silkscreen
40"x40" Special Arjomari paper
Printed by Jeff Wasserman

Edition: 200 plus 15 AP,
RTP, PPII, 3 GEL, SP, C

230 1970   EK70-330

Ellsworth Kelly
Blue/Yellow/Red

3 color lithograph
42½"x30" Special Arjomari paper
Printed by Andrew Vlady

Edition: 75 plus 9 AP,
TP, RTP, PPII, 3 GEL, C

231 1970   EK70-331

Ellsworth Kelly
Red Orange/Yellow/Blue

3 color lithograph
42½"x30" Special Arjomari paper
Printed by Ron Olds

Edition: 75 plus 9 AP,
TP, RTP, PPII, 3 GEL, C

232 1970   EK70-333

Ellsworth Kelly
Black/White/Black

3 color lithograph
42½"x30" Special Arjomari paper
Printed by Ron Adams

Edition: 75 plus 9 AP,
TP, RTP, PPII, 3 GEL, C

233 1970   EK70-335

Ellsworth Kelly
Orange/Green

2 color lithograph
41½"x30¼" Special Arjomari paper
Printed by George Page

Edition: 75 plus 9 AP,
TP, RTP, PPII, 3 GEL, C

234 1970   EK70-336

Ellsworth Kelly
Blue/Green

2 color lithograph
39½"x37¾" Special Arjomari paper
Printed by Dan Freeman

Edition: 75 plus 9 AP,
TP, RTP, PPII, 3 GEL, C

235 1970   EK70-340

Ellsworth Kelly
Yellow/Red Orange

2 color lithograph
35¼"x36¼" Special Arjomari paper
Printed by Stuart Henderson

Edition: 75 plus 9 AP,
TP, RTP, PPII, 3 GEL, C

236 1970   EK70-341

Ellsworth Kelly
Blue/Black

2 color lithograph
36"x34½" Special Arjomari paper
Printed by Charles Ritt

Edition: 75 plus 9 AP,
TP, RTP, PPII, 3 GEL, C

237 1970   EK70-343

Ellsworth Kelly
Black/Green

2 color lithograph
23¼"x19" Special Arjomari paper
Printed by Ron McPherson

Edition: 75 plus 9 AP,
TP, RTP, PPII, 3 GEL, C

238 1970   EK70-344

Ellsworth Kelly
Yellow/Black

2 color lithograph
41⅜"x36" Special Arjomari paper
Printed by Timothy Huchthausen

Edition: 75 plus 9 AP,
TP, RTP, PPII, 3 GEL, SP, C

239 1970   EK70-345

Ellsworth Kelly
Yellow/Orange

2 color lithograph
35"x41⅜" Special Arjomari paper
Printed by Paul Clinton

Edition: 75 plus 9 AP,
TP, RTP, PPII, 3 GEL, C

240 1970 EK70-364

Ellsworth Kelly
Red Orange over Black

2 color silkscreen
25"x30" Special Arjomari paper
Printed by Jeff Wasserman

Edition: 250 plus 25 AP,
RTP, PPII, 3 GEL, C

241 1970 RL70-328

Roy Lichtenstein
Peace Through Chemistry II

5 color lithograph/silkscreen
37¼"x63" Special Arjomari paper
Printed by Charles Ritt

Edition: 43 plus 7 AP,
RTP, PPII, 3 GEL, C

MODERN HEAD SERIES (242 TO 247)

242 1970 RL70-243

Roy Lichtenstein
Modern Head #1

4 color woodcut
24"x19" Hoshi paper
Printed by Richard Royce

Edition: 100 plus 7 AP,
RTP, PPII, 3 GEL, C

243 1970 RL70-245

Roy Lichtenstein
Modern Head #2

2 color lithograph and zinc line-cut
embossed
24½"x18½" Handmade Waterleaf paper
Printed by George Page

Edition: 100 plus 7 AP,
RTP, PPII, 3 GEL, C

244 1970 RL70-246

Roy Lichtenstein
Modern Head #3

1 color zinc line-cut embossed
24½"x18½" Handmade Waterleaf paper
Printed by George Page

Edition: 100 plus 7 AP,
RTP, PPII, 3 GEL, SP, C

245 1970 RL70-247

Roy Lichtenstein
Modern Head #4

7 color engraved, anodized and
printed aluminum
20¾"x17¼" with aluminum frame
Collaborator: Kenneth Tyler

Edition: 100 plus 7 AP,
RTP, PPII, 3 GEL, C

246 1970 RL70-244

Roy Lichtenstein
Modern Head #5

Embossed graphite
composition with
die-cut paper overlay
28"x19½" graphite composition,
Strathmore paper, wood and
enameled aluminum frame
Printed by George Page

Edition: 100 plus 7 AP,
RTP, PPII, 3 GEL, C

247 1970 RL70-2006

Roy Lichtenstein
Modern Head Relief

3-dimensional object
24"x17¾"x¾" solid brass
Collaborators: Kenneth Tyler,
Jeff Sanders, Bob McCullough

Edition: 100
Signature, edition no., chop,
copyright on copper plate on back

248 1970 RL70-368

Roy Lichtenstein
Chem IA

2 color silkscreen
30"x20⅜" Special Arjomari paper
Printed by Jeff Wasserman

Edition: 100 plus 10 AP,
RTP, PPII, 3 GEL, C

COPPER SERIES
(249 TO 255)

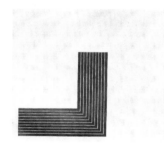

249 1970 FS70-320

Frank Stella
Creede II

3 color lithograph/silkscreen
16"x22" Special Arjomari paper
Printed by Paul Clinton

Edition: 70 plus 7 AP,
RTP, PPII, 3 GEL, C

250 1970 FS70-322

Frank Stella
Creede I

3 color lithograph/silkscreen
16"x22" Special Arjomari paper
Printed by Timothy Huchthausen

Edition: 70 plus 7 AP,
RTP, PPII, 3 GEL, C

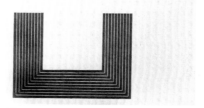

251 1970 FS70-323

Frank Stella
Lake City

3 color lithograph/silkscreen
16"x22" Special Arjomari paper
Printed by Timothy Huchthausen

Edition: 75 plus 7 AP,
RTP, PPII, 3 GEL, C

252 1970 FS70-324

Frank Stella
Telluride

3 color lithograph/silkscreen
16"x22" Special Arjomari paper
Printed by Paul Clinton

Edition: 75 plus 7 AP,
RTP, PPII, 3 GEL, C

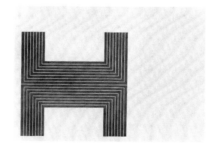

253 1970 FS70-325

Frank Stella
Pagosa Springs

3 color lithograph/silkscreen
16"x22" Special Arjomari paper
Printed by Paul Clinton

Edition: 75 plus 7 AP,
RTP, PPII, 3 GEL, C

254 1970 FS70-326

Frank Stella
Ouray

3 color lithograph/silkscreen
16"x22" Special Arjomari paper
Printed by Timothy Huchthausen

Edition: 70 plus 7 AP,
RTP, PPII, 3 GEL, C

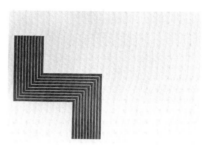

255 1970 FS70-327

Frank Stella
Ophir

3 color lithograph/silkscreen
16"x22" Special Arjomari paper
Printed by Paul Clinton

Edition: 75 plus 7 AP,
RTP, PPII, 3 GEL, C

256 1970 RR70-350

Robert Rauschenberg
Earth Day

7 color lithograph/collage
52½"x37½" Rives paper
Printed by Timothy Huchthausen

Edition: 50 plus 6 AP,
RTP, PPII, 3 GEL, SP, C

257 1970   CO70-2003

Claes Oldenburg
Double-Nose/Purse/Punching Bag/
Ashtray

3-dimensional object
10⅞"x20¾"x8⅜" leather, bronze, wood
Collaborators: Kenneth Tyler, Jeff
Sanders

Edition: 75 plus 3 AC, 3 PC
Signature, edition no., chop, copyright
stamped in bronze

258 1970   CO70-2003A

Claes Oldenburg
A History of the Double-Nose/
Purse/Punching Bag/Ashtray Multiple

4½"x3¼" leather covered book
Printed by letterpress on Byron
Thinpaque paper by Vernon Simpson,
leather cover by Jack Gray

Edition: 200 plus 25 AP, RTP, 3 GEL
1/200A to 75/200A included in multiple.
76/200B to 200/200B reserved for
future publication.

259 1970   CO70-369

Claes Oldenburg
Double-Nose/Purse/Punching Bag/
Ashtray

1 color lithograph
21"x19" Rives BFK paper
Printed by Kenneth Tyler

Edition: 50 plus 6 AP, 3 TP, RTP, 3 GEL, C

260 1970   AA69-305

Anni Albers
TRIII

1 color embossed silkscreen
16½"x 18½" Handmade Waterleaf
paper
Printed by George Page

Edition: 60 plus 6 AP,
RTP, PPII, 3 GEL, C

CARDBIRD SERIES (261 TO 262)

261 1971   RR71-2015

Robert Rauschenberg
Cardbird Door

3-dimensional object
80"x30"x11" corrugated cardboard,
Kraft paper, tape, wood, metal, photo
offset and screen printing
Collaborators: Kenneth Tyler, Jeff
Sanders, Jeff Wasserman

Edition: 25 plus 2 AC, 3 PC
Signature, edition no., chop, copyright
below door handle

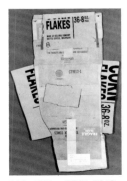

262 1971   RR71-2016

Robert Rauschenberg
Cardbird I

Collage print
45"x30" corrugated cardboard, tape,
photo offset and screen printing
Collaborators: Kenneth Tyler, Jeff
Wasserman

Edition: 75 plus 6 AP,
RTP, PPII, 3 GEL, SP, C
Signature, edition no., chop, copyright
under top flap

263 1971   EK71-5001

Ellsworth Kelly
Four Panels

4 color silkscreen
36¾"x62" Special Arjomari paper
Printed by Jeff Wasserman

Edition: 50 plus 9 AP,
RTP, PPII, 3 GEL, C

264 1971   EK71-5000

Ellsworth Kelly
Blue, Yellow and Red Squares

3 color silkscreen
34"x82" Special Arjomari paper
Printed by Jeff Wasserman

Edition: 50 plus 9 AP,
RTP, PPII, 3 GEL, C

265 1971   EK70-332

Ellsworth Kelly
Blue/White/Red

3 color lithograph
42½"x30" Special Arjomari paper
Printed by Andrew Vlady

Edition: 54 plus 9 AP,
RTP, PPII, 3 GEL, C

266 1971   EK70-346

Ellsworth Kelly
Blue/Red Orange/Green

3 color lithograph
42½"x30" Special Arjomari paper
Printed by Dan Freeman

Edition: 64 plus 9 AP,
RTP, PPII, 3 GEL, C

CUBE SERIES (267 TO 269)

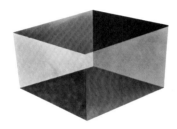

267 1971   RD71-2025

Ron Davis
Cube I

5 color photo offset on S.D. Warren
paper with laminated mylar overlay
and mounted on plastic
30"x40"
Collaborators: Kenneth Tyler, Jeff
Sanders

Edition: 100 plus 13 AP,
RTP, PPII, 3 GEL, C
Signature, edition no., chop, copyright
on label mounted on back of print

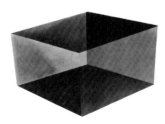

268 1971   RD71-2026

Ron Davis
Cube II

5 color photo offset on S.D. Warren
paper with laminated mylar overlay
and mounted on plastic
30"x40"

Collaborators: Kenneth Tyler, Jeff
Sanders

Edition: 114 plus 14 AP,
RTP, PPII, 3 GEL, C

Signature, edition no., chop, copyright
on label mounted on back of print

269 1971   RD71-2027

Ron Davis
Cube III

5 color photo offset on S.D. Warren
paper with laminated mylar overlay
and mounted on plastic
30"x40"

Collaborators: Kenneth Tyler, Jeff
Sanders

Edition: 125 plus 14 AP,
RTP, PPII, 3 GEL, C

Signature, edition no., chop, copyright
on label mounted on back of print

NEWFOUNDLAND SERIES (270 TO 275)

270 1971   FS70-359

Frank Stella
River of Ponds I

11 color lithograph
38"x38" Special Arjomari paper
Printed by James Webb

Edition: 78 plus 10 AP,
RTP, PPII, 3 GEL, C

271 1971   FS70-357

Frank Stella
River of Ponds II

8 color lithograph
38"x38" Special Arjomari paper
Printed by Dan Freeman

Edition: 78 plus 10 AP,
RTP, PPII, 3 GEL, C

101

272 1971   FS70-356

Frank Stella
River of Ponds III

9 color lithograph
38"x38" Special Arjomari paper
Printed by Ron Olds

Edition: 75 plus 10 AP,
RTP, PPII, 3 GEL, C

273 1971   FS70-355

Frank Stella
River of Ponds IV

11 color lithograph
38"x38" Special Arjomari paper
Printed by Ron McPherson

Edition: 70 plus 10 AP,
RTP, PPII, 3 GEL, C

274 1971   FS70-360

Frank Stella
Port aux Basques

14 color lithograph/silkscreen
38″x70″ Special Arjomari paper
Printed by George Page, Andrew
Vlady, Jeff Wasserman

Edition: 58 plus 10 AP, 7 TP,
RTP, PPII, 3 GEL, C

275 1971   FS70-361

Frank Stella
Bonne Bay

14 color lithograph/silkscreen
38″x70″ Special Arjomari paper
Printed by Stuart Henderson, Ron
McPherson, Jeff Wasserman

Edition: 58 plus 12 AP,
2 TP, RTP, PPII, 3 GEL, C

276 1971   JJ71-373

Jasper Johns
Target

2 color lithograph with collage and
rubber stamp in plexiglas and wood
box
Print: 12¼″x10″ Box: 13⅜″x11⅛″x1″
Printed by Kenneth Tyler

Edition: 50 plus 6 AP,
RTP, PPII, 3 GEL, C

*Offset edition with collage: 22,500
For exhibition catalogue,* Technics
and Creativity: Gemini G.E.L., *New York:
The Museum of Modern Art, 1971*

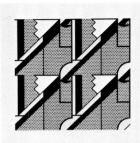

277 1971   RL71-363

Roy Lichtenstein
Modern Print

5 color lithograph/silkscreen
31″x31″ Special Arjomari paper
Printed by Timothy Huchthausen, Jeff
Wasserman

Edition: 200 plus 15 AP,
RTP, PPII, 3 GEL, C
*Edition for The Museum of
Modern Art, New York*

278 1971   JC71-2010

John Chamberlain
Le Molé

3-dimensional object
7″ (high) cast polyester resin covered
with an aluminum and silicon oxide
vapor deposit coating
Collaborators: Jeff Sanders, James Robie

Edition: 56 plus 3 AC, 3 PC
Signature, edition no., chop, copyright
on mounted plate

279 1971   EK71-2024

Edward Kienholz
Sawdy

3-dimensional object
39½″x36″x7″ car door, mirrored window,
automotive lacquer, polyester resin,
silkscreen, fluorescent light, galvanized
sheet metal
Collaborators: Kenneth Tyler, Jeff
Sanders, James Robie

Edition: 50 plus 2 AC, 3 PC
Signature, edition no., chop, copyright
on sticker mounted on side of door

280 1971   CO71-2005

Claes Oldenburg
Ice Bag—Scale B

Programmed kinetic sculpture
48″ diameter rising to 40″
Yellow nylon material, fiberglass,
mechanical movement
Collaborators: Kenneth Tyler, Jeff
Sanders, Lou Faibish, Frank Doose

Edition: 25
Signature, edition no., chop, copyright
on metal plate mounted inside

281 1971   CO71-2011

Claes Oldenburg
Geometric Mouse—Scale C

Movable 3-dimensional object
24½″x20″ (9″ ear) black anodized
aluminum
Collaborators: Kenneth Tyler, Jeff
Sanders, Lou Faibish, Frank Doose

Edition: 120 plus 3 AC, 3 PC
Signature, edition no., chop, copyright
on disc attached to chain

282 1971   JA71-383

Josef Albers
White Embossing on Gray I

1 color line-cut embossed
26⅛″x20⅛″ Roleaf paper
Printed by George Page

Edition: 125 plus 9 AP,
RTP, PPII, 3 GEL, C

283 1971   EK71-2007
Ellsworth Kelly
Mirrored Concorde

3-dimensional object
22¾″x26½″x1″ chromed steel
Collaborators: Kenneth Tyler,
Jeff Sanders

In production: edition size to be
determined.
Signature, edition no., chop, copyright
on plate on base

284 1971   DJ71-2028
Don Judd
Untitled

3-dimensional object
4″x23″x27″ stainless steel,
brown acrylic sheet
Collaborators: Kenneth Tyler,
Jeff Sanders

In production: edition size to be
determined.

285 1971   CO71-2008
Claes Oldenburg
Ice Bag—Scale C

Programmed kinetic sculpture
12′ diameter rising to 10′
Blue nylon material, fiberglass,
mechanical movement
Collaborators: Kenneth Tyler, Jeff
Sanders, Lou Faibish, Frank Doose

In production: edition limited to 4

INDEX OF ARTISTS

103

SELECTED BIBLIOGRAPHY

Articles and Reviews

Baker, Kenneth. "Bread." *Christian Science Monitor* (Los Angeles), October 19, 1970, p. 8.

Coplans, John. "The Artist Speaks: Claes Oldenburg." *Art in America* (New York), March-April 1969, pp. 68-75.

_____. "Roy Lichtenstein's New Prints: an Interview with John Coplans." *Studio International* (London), December 1970, pp. 263-265, 269.

Danieli, Fidel A. "Los Angeles." *Artforum* (Los Angeles), January 1967, pp. 62-63.

Davis, Douglas M. "Rauschenberg's Recent Graphics." *Art in America* (New York), July-August 1969, pp. 90-95.

Forst, Robert. "A Heart of Stone." *Western Printer & Lithographer* (Los Angeles), April 1968, pp. 16-17.

Glueck, Grace. "Movable Object, Irresistible Force." *New York Times*, May 4, 1969, p. D-23.

Hughes, Robert. "Art." *Time* (New York), January 18, 1971, pp. 56-57.

Karshan, Donald H. "American Printmaking 1670-1968." *Art in America* (New York), July-August 1968, pp. 48, 50, 53.

Levinson, Robert S. "Art Scene." *Coast FM & Fine Arts* (Los Angeles), May 1969, p. 12-13.

_____. "Art Scene." *Coast FM & Fine Arts* (Los Angeles), July 1970, pp. 18-19.

_____. "Gemini and the Rebirth of Graphics." *Los Angeles Times, West Magazine*, January 24, 1971, pp. 24-29.

_____. "Levinson's Lesson in Litho Largesse." *FM & Fine Arts* (Los Angeles), October 1968, p. 33.

_____. "Renaissance of Lithography." *Westways* (Los Angeles), November 1970, pp. 6-10, 52.

Nakahara, Usuke. "Claes Oldenburg: Desire for Giant Things." *Monthly Art Magazine, Bijutsu Techo* (Japan), November 1969, pp. 91-137.

"Original Art, Hot Off the Presses," *Life* (New York), January 23, 1970, pp. 57-61.

Raphael, Shirley. "Research in the Graphic Arts." *Vie des Arts* (Montreal), Summer 1970, pp. 50-51.

_____. "Revival in Graphics." *Art* (Toronto), Spring 1970, p. 4.

"The Revival of Lithography." *Architectural Digest* (Los Angeles), March-April 1971, pp. 4, 68-77.

Richard, Paul. "Apollo 11 as an Art Form." *Washington Post*, October 30, 1970, p. D1.

Richardson, Brenda. "It Breathes, It Creeps —It's Ice Bag." *San Francisco Sunday Examiner & Chronicle*, February 22, 1970, pp. 42-43.

Rose, Barbara. "The Airflow Multiple of Claes Oldenburg." *Studio International* (London), June 1970, pp. 254-255.

_____. "The Graphic Work of Jasper Johns, Part I." *Artforum* (New York), March 1970, pp. 39-45.

_____. "The Graphic Art of Jasper Johns, Part II." *Artforum* (New York), September 1970, pp. 65-74.

_____. "The Print Revival." *Vogue* (New York), September 1968, p. 274.

Seidenbaum, Art. "Lithography Art Leaves Its Print." *Los Angeles Times*, December 14, 1967, p. IV-1.

Sherman, John K. "Artist Combines Dream Reality." *Minneapolis Tribune*, February 5, 1967, p. 12.

Sherrill, Robert. "Gemini G.E.L." *Lithopinion* (New York), Summer 1970, pp. 50-63.

"Sort of a Commercial for an Ice Bag: The Latest Work of Claes Oldenburg," *Lumière* (Melbourne), July 1970, pp. 21-22.

Stengel, R. F. "Simple Drive System Generates Complex Motion." *Design News* (Los Angeles), April 13, 1970, p. 67.

Tono, Yoshiaki. "Robert Rauschenberg: His Life Story." *Monthly Art Magazine, Bijutsu Techo* (Japan), April 1970, pp. 68-96.

Tuten, Fred [eric]. "People Are Talking About." *Vogue* (New York), June 1969, p. 120.

Von Meier, Kurt. "Los Angeles." *Art International* (Zurich), October 1967, pp. 60-61.

Wilson, William. "A Big Cure for America's Image." *Los Angeles Times*, January 12, 1970, pp. 1,6.

_____. "Another Art Look at Johns, Oldenburg." *Los Angeles Times*, December 1, 1969, p. IV-17.

Young, Joseph E. "Claes Oldenburg at Gemini." *Artist's Proof* (New York), vol. 9, 1969, pp. 44-52.

_____. "Jasper Johns: An Appraisal." *Art International* (Zurich), September 1969, pp. 50-56.

_____. "Jasper Johns Lead-Relief Prints." *Artist's Proof* (New York), vol.10, 1971, pp.36-38.

_____. "Lichtenstein: Printmaker." *Art and Artists* (London), March 1970, pp. 50-53.

_____. "Los Angeles." *Art International* (Zurich), March 1970, pp. 83-84, 87.

Gemini G.E.L. Brochures

Coplans, John. *Ellsworth Kelly*. 1970.

_____. *Frank Stella: The V Series*. 1968.

Hopkins, Henry. *Jasper Johns: Figures*. 1968.

Josef Albers: White Line Squares, Series I of Eight Lithographs. 1967.

Josef Albers: White Line Squares, Series II of Eight Lithographs. 1967.

Leider, Philip. *Frank Stella: Star of Persia I & II, Black Series I*. 1967.

Lippard, Lucy R. *Robert Rauschenberg: Booster and 7 Studies*. 1967.

Man Ray. 1967.

Nodelman, Sheldon, and Tyler, Kenneth E. *Josef Albers: Embossed Linear Constructions.* 1969.

Rose, Barbara. *Claes Oldenburg: Notes.* 1968.

———. *Claes Oldenburg: Profile Airflow.* 1970.

———. *Figurine Cups by Ken Price.* 1970.

Solomon, Alan. *Jasper Johns: Lead Reliefs.* 1969.

Sort of a Commercial for an Ice Bag. 1970.

Tuten, Frederic. *Lichtenstein at Gemini.* 1969.

Whitney, David. *Robert Rauschenberg: Reels (B + C).* 1968.

William Crutchfield: Americana. 1967.

Exhibition Catalogues
(arranged chronologically)

Los Angeles. Los Angeles County Museum of Art. *Josef Albers: White Line Squares.* October 28-January 1, 1967. Foreword and Acknowledgments by Kenneth E. Tyler. Essays by Josef Albers and Henry T. Hopkins.

San Diego. University of California San Diego Art Gallery. *Lithographs from Gemini.* October 4-November 3, 1968. Essay by Paul Brach.

San Antonio. San Antonio Art League, San Antonio Museum Association, Witte Memorial Museum. *Lithographs, Gemini G.E.L.* October 13-November 10, 1968. Essay by Kurt von Meier.

Davis. Memorial Union Art Gallery, University of California. *Lithographs from Gemini.* August 4-September 12, 1969. Essay by Frederic Tuten. Roy Lichtenstein's Rouen Cathedral and Haystacks series.

Los Angeles. Los Angeles County Museum of Art. *Recent Prints from Gemini.* October 7, 1969-January 4, 1970. Essay by Joseph E. Young.

Philadelphia. Institute of Contemporary Art, University of Pennsylvania. *Rauschenberg: Graphic Art.* April 1-May 10, 1970. Introduction by Lawrence Alloway.

Philadelphia. Philadelphia Museum of Art. *Jasper Johns: Prints 1960-1970.* April 1-May 10, 1970. Essay by Richard S. Field.

Minneapolis. The Minneapolis Institute of Arts. *Robert Rauschenberg Prints 1948/1970.* August 6-September 27, 1970. Foreword and Introduction by Edward A. Foster.

Hannover. Kunstverein Hannover. *Robert Rauschenberg.* August 29-September 27, 1970. Essays by Lucy R. Lippard, Lawrence Alloway, Douglas M. Davis.

Irvine. University of California. *Roy Lichtenstein: Graphics, Reliefs & Sculpture 1969-1970.* October 27-December 6, 1970. Preface and Interview by John Coplans. Published by University of California and Gemini G.E.L.

New York. The Museum of Modern Art. *Jasper Johns Lithographs.* December 22-March 21, 1971. Essay by Riva Castleman.

CHECKLIST OF THE EXHIBITION

The Museum of Modern Art, New York
May 5-July 6, 1971

Complete data on each work will be
found in the Catalogue Raisonné under
the number given in parentheses. Page
numbers in italics refer to illustrations.

Josef Albers
American, born Germany 1888

1. White Line Square I. 1966. (2)
The Museum of Modern Art, John B.
Turner Fund

2. White Line Square II. 1966. (3)
The Museum of Modern Art, John B.
Turner Fund

3. White Line Square IV. 1966. (5)
The Museum of Modern Art, John B.
Turner Fund

4. White Line Square VII. 1966. (8)
The Museum of Modern Art, John B.
Turner Fund

5. White Line Square VIII. 1966. (9).
page 32
The Museum of Modern Art, John B.
Turner Fund

6. White Line Square IX. 1966. (10)
The Museum of Modern Art, John B.
Turner Fund

7. White Line Square XIV. 1966. (15)
The Museum of Modern Art, John B.
Turner Fund

8. White Line Square XV. 1966. (16).
page 33 The Museum of Modern Art,
John B. Turner Fund

9. Embossed Linear Construction 2-A.
1969. (138) The Museum of Modern Art,
gift of Gemini G.E.L.

10. Embossed Linear Construction 2-C.
1969. (140) The Museum of Modern Art,
gift of Gemini G.E.L.

11. White Embossing on Gray I. 1971.
(282). *page 34* The Museum of Modern Art,
gift of Gemini G.E.L.

John Chamberlain
American, born 1927

12. Le Molé. 1971. (278). *page 69*
Collection Gemini G.E.L.

Ron Davis
American, born 1937

13. Cube III. 1971. (269). *page 62*
The Museum of Modern Art, gift of Dr.
and Mrs. Judd Marmor

Jasper Johns
American, born 1930

COLOR NUMERAL SERIES (14-23).
pages 36-37

14. Figure 0. 1969. (116). *page 36*
The Museum of Modern Art, gift of Gemini
G.E.L.

15. Figure 1. 1969. (117). *page 36*
Collection Gemini G.E.L.

16. Figure 2. 1969. (118). *page 36*
Collection Gemini G.E.L.

17. Figure 3. 1969. (119). *page 36*
Collection Gemini G.E.L.

18. Figure 4. 1969. (120). *page 36*
Collection Gemini G.E.L.

19. Figure 5. 1969. (121). *page 37*
Collection Gemini G.E.L.

20. Figure 6. 1969. (122). *page 37*
Collection Gemini G.E.L.

21. Figure 7. 1969. (123). *pages 35, 37*
The Museum of Modern Art, gift of Gemini
G.E.L.

22. Figure 8. 1969. (124). *page 37*
Collection Gemini G.E.L.

23. Figure 9. 1969. (125). *page 37*
The Museum of Modern Art, gift of Gemini
G.E.L.

24. No. 1969. (128). *page 38* The Museum
of Modern Art, gift of Philip Johnson

25. Flag. 1969. (131) Collection Gemini G.E.L.

26. Light Bulb. 1969. (132). *page 39*
The Museum of Modern Art, gift of
David Steinmetz

27. Numerals. 1970. (189)
Collection Gemini G.E.L.

28. Fragment-According to What-Bent
"Blue." 1971. (not in Catalogue Raisonné)
4 color lithograph, 25½" x 28¾"
Collection Gemini G.E.L.

Don Judd
American, born 1928

29. Untitled. 1971. (284). *page 63*
Collection Gemini G.E.L.

Ellsworth Kelly
American, born 1923

30. Blue/Yellow/Red. 1970. (230)
page 65 The Museum of Modern Art,
gift of Connie and Jack Glenn
and Pinky and Arthur Kase

31. Black/White/Black. 1970. (232)
The Museum of Modern Art, gift of
Connie and Jack Glenn and Pinky and
Arthur Kase

32. Orange/Green. 1970. (233)
The Museum of Modern Art, gift of
Connie and Jack Glenn and Pinky and
Arthur Kase

33. Blue/Green. 1970. (234). *page 66*
The Museum of Modern Art, gift of
Connie and Jack Glenn and Pinky and
Arthur Kase

34. Yellow/Red Orange. 1970. (235)
The Museum of Modern Art, gift of
Connie and Jack Glenn and Pinky and
Arthur Kase

35. Blue/Black. 1970. (236)
The Museum of Modern Art, gift of
Connie and Jack Glenn and Pinky and
Arthur Kase

36. Yellow/Black. 1970. (238)
The Museum of Modern Art, gift of
Connie and Jack Glenn and Pinky and
Arthur Kase

37. Yellow/Orange. 1970. (239)
The Museum of Modern Art, gift of
Connie and Jack Glenn and Pinky and
Arthur Kase

38. Four Panels. 1971. (263). *page 67*
Collection Gemini G.E.L.

39. Mirrored Concorde. 1971. (283).
page 64 Collection Gemini G.E.L.

Edward Kienholz
American, born 1927

40. Sawdy. 1971. (279). *page 68*
Collection Gemini G.E.L.

Roy Lichtenstein
American, born 1923

41. Cathedral #1. 1969. (142)
The Museum of Modern Art, gift of
Mr. and Mrs. David Gensburg

42. Cathedral #2. 1969. (143)
The Museum of Modern Art, gift of
Mr. and Mrs. David Gensburg

43. Cathedral #3. 1969. (144)
The Museum of Modern Art, gift of
Mr. and Mrs. David Gensburg

44. Cathedral #4. 1969. (145)
The Museum of Modern Art, gift of
Mr. and Mrs. David Gensburg

45. Cathedral #5. 1969. (146). *page 41*
The Museum of Modern Art, gift of
Mr. and Mrs. David Gensburg

46. Cathedral #6. 1969. (147)
The Museum of Modern Art, gift of
Mr. and Mrs. David Gensburg

47. Peace Through Chemistry I. 1970.
(190). *page 43*
The Museum of Modern Art, promised
gift of Mr. and Mrs. Donald B. Marron

48. Peace Through Chemistry Bronze.
1970. (222). *page 42*
Collection Gemini G.E.L.

49. Modern Head #3. 1970. (244).
page 44
The Museum of Modern Art, gift of
Mrs. Portia Harcus

50. Modern Head Relief. 1970. (247).
page 45
Collection Gemini G.E.L.

51. Modern Print. 1971. (277)
The Museum of Modern Art, gift of
the artist

Claes Oldenburg
American, born Sweden 1929

52. Profile Airflow. 1969. (178). *page 57*
The Museum of Modern Art, gift of
John and Kimiko Powers

53. Sort of a Commercial for an Ice Bag
Film directed by Michel Hugo. 1970.
(181). *page 61*
Collection Gemini G.E.L.

54. Double-Nose/Purse/Punching Bag/
Ashtray. 1970. (257). *pages 58-59*
Collection Gemini G.E.L.

55. Ice Bag—Scale B. 1971. (280).
page 60
Collection Gemini G.E.L.

56. Geometric Mouse—Scale C. 1971.
(281). *page 56*
Collection Gemini G.E.L.

57. Ice Bag—Scale C. 1971. (285)
Collection Gemini G.E.L.

Ken Price
American, born 1935

58. Figurine Cup V. 1970. (197)
The Museum of Modern Art, gift of
Gemini G.E.L.

59. Figurine Cup VI. 1970. (198). *page 40*
The Museum of Modern Art, gift of
Gemini G.E.L. .

Robert Rauschenberg
American, born 1925

60. Test Stone #5A. 1967. (31). *page 46*
The Museum of Modern Art, John B.
Turner Fund

61. Booster. 1967. (32). *page 47*
The Museum of Modern Art, John B.
Turner Fund

62. Test Stone #6. 1967. (33)
The Museum of Modern Art, John B.
Turner Fund

63. Test Stone #7. 1967. (34)
The Museum of Modern Art, John B.
Turner Fund

64. Horn. 1969. (162). *page 48*
The Museum of Modern Art, gift of
Dorothy and Lou Faibish

65. Sack. 1969. (166)
The Museum of Modern Art, gift of
Dorothy and Lou Faibish

66. Earth Crust. 1969. (169)
Collection Gemini G.E.L.

67. Banner. 1969. (173)
Collection Gemini G.E.L.

68. Waves. 1969. (174)
Collection Gemini G.E.L.

69. Sky Garden, 1969. (175). *page 49*
The Museum of Modern Art, gift of
Mr. and Mrs. Victor W. Ganz

70. Sky Garden (color trial proof).
1969. (175)
Collection Gemini G.E.L.

71. Tilt. 1970. (188)
Collection Gemini G.E.L.

72. Tracks. 1970. (200). *page 50*
The Museum of Modern Art, gift of
Donald Karshan

73. Air Pocket. 1970. (203)
The Museum of Modern Art, gift of
Tomas del Amo

74. Cardbird Door. 1971. (261). *page 51*
Collection Gemini G.E.L.

Frank Stella
American, born 1936

75. Star of Persia I. 1967. (46). *page 52*
The Museum of Modern Art, John B.
Turner Fund

76. Star of Persia II. 1967. (47)
The Museum of Modern Art, John B.
Turner Fund

77. Irving Blum Memorial Edition. 1967.
(74)
Collection Gemini G.E.L.

78. Quathlamba II. 1968. (80). *page 53*
The Museum of Modern Art, John B.
Turner Fund

79. Empress of India I. 1968. (81). *page 53*
The Museum of Modern Art, John B.
Turner Fund

80. Empress of India II. 1968. (82)
The Museum of Modern Art, John B.
Turner Fund

81. Grid Stack. 1970. (225). *page 54*
Collection Gemini G.E.L.

82. Pastel Stack. 1970. (227)
The Museum of Modern Art, gift of
Sam and Edna Neidorf

83. River of Ponds III. 1971. (272)
Collection Gemini G.E.L.

84. Port aux Basques. 1971. (274).
page 55
Collection Gemini G.E.L.